FCE REVISED Result

Teacher's Pack

DAVID BAKER

OXFORD
UNIVERSITY PRESS

OXFORD
UNIVERSITY PRESS

Great Clarendon Street, Oxford OX2 6DP

Oxford University Press is a department of the University of Oxford.
It furthers the University's objective of excellence in research, scholarship,
and education by publishing worldwide in

Oxford New York

Auckland Cape Town Dar es Salaam Hong Kong Karachi
Kuala Lumpur Madrid Melbourne Mexico City Nairobi
New Delhi Shanghai Taipei Toronto

With offices in

Argentina Austria Brazil Chile Czech Republic France Greece
Guatemala Hungary Italy Japan Poland Portugal Singapore
South Korea Switzerland Thailand Turkey Ukraine Vietnam

OXFORD and OXFORD ENGLISH are registered trade marks of
Oxford University Press in the UK and in certain other countries

ISBN: 978 0 19 481738 7

Printed in China

This book is printed on paper from certified and well-managed sources.

Contents

Introduction

Course overview

FCE Result (revised edition 2011) is a contemporary and attractively designed course with unusual, eye-catching artwork. It covers the major language skills, and provides students with comprehensive preparation for *Cambridge English: First* at the Council of Europe B2 level. Its lively, up-to-date texts are taken from authentic sources, such as newspapers, magazines, brochures and books, and include interviews and radio programmes. Its engaging topics are designed to stimulate interest and provoke discussion.

Each unit of the course has a general topic heading, but each section within the unit is free-standing and has a different angle on the overall topic. This gives teachers flexibility in planning lessons and provides variety for students. There is an emphasis on grammar and vocabulary work throughout the course and a review section at the end of each unit which allows students to check what they have learned. Dictionary skills work is integrated throughout the Student's Book and Workbook, with additional support in the *Using a dictionary for exams* booklet in the Teacher's Pack (see page 10 of this Introduction).

As well as being encouraged to consolidate, improve and activate their knowledge of the English language, students are given extensive training in all the examination skills and task types. The *How to do it* boxes offer general help in tackling these task types, and in building on their language skills, while the *Tip* boxes give additional helpful hints on how to approach individual tasks.

The flexibility, organisation and additional components of the course enable it to be used with students studying several hours a week throughout the academic year, or with students on shorter, more intensive courses.

The course consists of a Student's Book with or without Online Skills Practice plus online practice test, two class audio cds, a Teacher's Pack, Workbook Resource Packs (with or without key), and iTools (classroom material for use on interactive whiteboards).

Course components

The Student's Book

The course consists of 12 units, each of which is divided into these sections:

- Lead in
- Reading
- Vocabulary
- Grammar
- Listening
- Speaking
- Use of English
- Vocabulary
- Writing
- Review

The Lead in sections are designed to introduce, through a variety of skills input and activities, the various sub-topics and key vocabulary of the unit. The Reading sections deal comprehensively with all the Reading task types. There is a short lead in question before students tackle the exam task and sometimes a short exercise based on the vocabulary in the text itself, although students are not encouraged to find out the precise meaning of all the words in the text. The last exercise often invites students to react to what they have just read.

The Vocabulary sections draw on and expand topic or lexico-grammatical vocabulary from the Lead in, Reading or Use of English pages, and encourage students to use the vocabulary in context. As well as topic-related vocabulary, there are functional phrases, useful expressions, easily confused words, word formation tasks and phrasal verbs. Many of these sections encourage students to refer to a dictionary, and a number of exercises are designed to show students how a dictionary can help specifically with exam tasks, as well as generally supporting their language learning, and helping them to become more independent learners.

The Grammar sections adopt a holistic approach to grammar, tackling general areas by checking what students already know, and then inviting them to practise newly acquired knowledge. The sections are cross-referenced to the Grammar Reference at the back of the Student's Book.

The Listening sections introduce the topic in question and encourage students to react to what they have heard. The tasks cover all the Listening task types and students are encouraged to build on their listening skills in a variety of ways, e.g. by deciding why answers are wrong. The revised edition of the Student's Book includes five replacement Listening tasks.

The Speaking sections focus on a particular part of the Speaking test. Many units have recorded models of the tasks for students to listen to, either to analyse them or to use as a model before doing the task themselves. As well as the *How to do it* boxes, help is also given in the form of groups of phrases which students can use when doing the tasks. Colourful artwork also appears in the form of illustrations or pictures used for the exam tasks. Wherever possible, the pictures have been given a prominent position on the page to facilitate their use for exam tasks.

As well as highlighting the individual task types, care has been taken to make the Use of English sections as interesting and stimulating as possible. Each section covers one or more of the five task types and most also focus on another aspect of language, e.g. spelling and punctuation, grammar or vocabulary. Dictionary skills work, similar to that in the vocabulary sections, also features here.

The Writing sections deal comprehensively with the compulsory Part 1 question and all the choices in the Part 2 examination task types. Models of good and less effective writing styles are given and students are invited to analyse these, practise their writing skills at sentence or paragraph level, then produce a complete piece of writing of their own.

The Review sections mainly test the key vocabulary and grammar studied in the unit. Several short exercises invite students to revise this material and identify any areas requiring further study. They provide a valuable progress check at regular intervals and can be done in class or set for homework, depending on the time available.

The Exam Overview outlines comprehensively what each part of the exam consists of, how long each paper lasts and the number of marks awarded, and explains the grading system or criteria for assessment, where applicable. Each paper is broken down into the following:

- the number of items, sections or task types in each part
- what you do in each part
- what each part tests

Cross-references to the *How to do it* boxes on the relevant pages of the Student's Book are given here.

The Appendix contains additional material for certain pages of the Student's Book.

The Writing Guide gives students additional support with further questions, model answers and guidance for writing letters and emails, magazine articles, reviews, essays, and reports.

The Grammar Reference provides comprehensive rules and explanations for the usage of individual grammar items, namely: articles, simple and continuous tenses, present tenses, talking about the future, talking about the past, verb patterns, reported speech, modals, passives, *so* and *such*, relative clauses, comparatives and superlatives, conditionals, and causatives.

Online Skills Practice

The Student's Book is also available with access to Online Skills Practice and an online practice test.

Using the Online Skills Practice

The Online Skills Practice is accessed via a unique 'unlock' code. This can be found on the card at the back of the Student's Book, in the Student's Book with Online Skills Practice Pack. The exercises and tasks in the Online Skills Practice allow students to continue to develop the skills and sub-skills they need for the exam outside class time.

The Online Skills Practice can be:

- **teacher-managed** via a free Learning Management System (follow the instructions for Option 1 or Option 2 on the card at the back of the Student's Book.)

OR

- used by individual students for **self-study** (refer your students to the instructions for Option 3 on the card at the back of the Student's Book).

Teacher-managed Online Skills Practice
If teaching the Student's Book in class, we recommend choosing this option in order to assign exercises and tasks from the Online Skills Practice and the online

practice test via the free Learning Management System (LMS), where it's easy to:

1 manage what exercises and tasks your students do and when they do them.
2 see your students' results in an online markbook so that you can identify areas of class or individual weakness, allowing you to focus on what students really need to work on.
3 read, comment on and mark your students' extended writing tasks online, with an option to return work to students for them to improve and resubmit. A marking guide and sample answer are provided.
4 listen to, comment on and mark your students' recorded responses to Speaking tasks online.

You can choose whether to assign the exercises and tasks in the Online Skills Practice 'without help' (for assessment) or 'with help' (for supported learning). For exercises and tasks you set 'with help', students are allowed to:

1 mark their answers, have another attempt at anything they got wrong, and see the correct answers with explanatory feedback.
2 look up the meaning of words in questions and texts in the integrated online *Oxford Advanced Learner's Dictionary*, 8th Edition. This saves time and helps students improve their vocabulary.
3 read tips and strategies to help them prepare for the exam.
4 see sample answers for the writing tasks and useful language for the Speaking tasks.

If you assign exercises 'without help', these support features will be disabled.

You could choose the sections or exercises of the Online Skills Practice you wish students to do, and assign them first 'without help', i.e. with all support features disabled. This will allow you to assess how well prepared your students are at any stage of the course. You can then assign any problematic exercises again 'with help', i.e. all support features enabled, so that individual students can benefit from the learning support features. You can assign all the Online Skills Practice, or one unit, or a selection of sections or exercises.

If you choose to use the LMS, we recommend following instructions for Option 1 on the card in the Student's Book. If you would prefer to register students yourself, you will need to collect their cards with unlock codes and follow the instructions for Option 2.

Self-study Online Skills Practice

You may prefer your students to work through the material in the Online Skills Practice and practice test at their own pace, using the 'self-study' option. Students will need an email address to register. They will need to follow the instructions for Option 3 on the card in their books. For this option, students will have access to all the learning support features (see below), but you will not be able to track their progress, see their results or do any marking online.

Note!

It is very important that you tell your students which access option you want to use. For more information about Online Practice Skills and the LMS go to www.oxfordenglishtesting.com.

Students have 1 year to complete the Online Skills Practice and Practice Test from the time they register.

Online Skills Practice content

Each of the 12 units in the Student's Book has four corresponding sections in the Online Skills Practice. Each of these sections starts with one or two sub-skills training exercises, and concludes with practice of an exam-type task for that skill/paper. These sections extend and build on the *Tip* and *How to do it* boxes, and the parts of each paper that are covered in the Student's Book units. The training exercises focus on the sub-skills and strategies that will help students with specific exam tasks.

Learning support features

These learning support features are available to students for assignments set 'with help' or if students are using the self-study option.

Feedback	Students get answers and explanatory feedback on automatically marked questions. If they can understand why they answered a question incorrectly it will help them to think more clearly about a similar question the next time.
Dictionary look-up: *Oxford Advanced Learner's Dictionary*, 8th Edition	Allows students to look up the meaning of words in exercises and texts.

Tips	Tips are available on how to answer exam questions and other general language learning tips. Students need to click 'Show Tip' on the left of their Online Skills Practice screen.
Audio scripts	Students can read audio scripts in the Listening and Speaking sections. They can view these by clicking the 'Audio script' link at the bottom of their Online Skills Practice screen.
Sample answers	Students can see sample answers in the Writing sections and read comments on them to see what is expected in the exam. Students can then improve their own answer.
Useful language	Lists of useful language are provided in the Speaking sections, accessed by clicking the 'Useful language' link at the bottom of the screen.
Change your answers and try again	Students can click the 'Change' button to try an exercise or answer a question again. If students are using the self-study option or you have set them the assignment 'with help', they can change their answers as many times as they wish before submitting their assignment.

Online practice test

The unlock code for the Online Skills Practice also includes access to a complete oxfordenglishtesting.com practice test. If you are using the LMS option you can assign this test to your students as a whole test, or by paper or part using *Test mode* (= 'without help') so that you can assess how well-prepared your students are, or in *Practice mode* (= 'with help') for practice and familiarisation with the exam task types.

iTools

FCE Result (revised) iTools provides teachers with new material for use on interactive whiteboards (IWBs). This aims to develop and extend material in the Student's Book. Please note that this iTools is <u>not</u> the Student's Book on screen. Each unit in the iTools corresponds to the topic and lexical/grammatical content of the Student's Book. The FCE Skills section provides further opportunities for students to develop their Reading, Use of English and Listening skills.

Content

Course-specific content
Three or four new exercises develop and expand on material in the corresponding Student's Book unit. These include vocabulary and grammar extension tasks, PowerPoint presentations of grammar points, additional reading and listening tasks for additional exam practice, photos for Speaking activities with additional tasks, and video clips.

The Writing Guides from the Student's Book are included for class use.

Skills practice
• Four interactive Reading skills tasks – focusing on sub-skills for Reading.

• Four interactive Use of English tasks (one for each part of the exam).

• Four interactive Listening tasks (one for each part of the exam).

Resources

The following are available via the *Resources* tab:

• Teacher's Book answer key

• *Speaking and Writing Assessment Booklet* (in PDF format)

• Teacher's DVD

• *Using a dictionary for exams* booklet (in PDF format)

• Student's Book audio

• Unit and Progress Tests – please note that these are additional to those printed in the Teacher's Book, and both versions of these tests are applicable to the revised Student's Book material.

The Teacher's Pack

The Teacher's Pack consists of a Teacher's Book with DVD, a *Writing and Speaking Assessment Booklet* and a *Using a dictionary for exams* booklet, updated in the revised edition to refer to the OALD 8th Edition.

The Teacher's Book contains procedural notes and a full answer key, including suggested answers, for the activities in the Student's Book. It also includes the tapescripts for the listening sections with highlighted answers, as well as optional activities for classroom use. There are 12 Unit Tests and four Progress Tests with answer keys, which can be photocopied for classroom use.

The 32-page *Writing and Speaking Assessment Booklet* is divided into two sections. The Writing section contains information about the assessment criteria used by Cambridge ESOL for marking Paper 2 answers, and has an authentic sample answer, written by a student studying at this level, for each of the tasks in the Writing sections of the Student's Book. Each answer is accompanied by notes on the requirements of the task, and an assessment of the answer according to the exam criteria.

The Speaking section specifically supports the DVD, which contains footage of real students doing Paper 5 tests under exam conditions, with commentaries and analysis by experienced oral examiners. The DVD is designed to help teachers in a number of ways: to familiarise them with the format of the Speaking Paper; to explain the requirements of each Part and the assessment criteria used by the examiners; to enable them to assess their own students and be able to train them to give a good performance. Sections of the DVD can also be shown in class to students, using the photocopiable worksheets in the booklet at the same time.

The 32-page *Using a dictionary for exams* booklet complements the dictionary work that features throughout the Student's Book and Workbook. It contains ideas for classroom activities for each of the main papers in the *Cambridge English: Preliminary, First* and *Advanced* exams, showing how dictionaries can help with specific exam tasks. The 11 worksheets are photocopiable for use in class.

The Workbook Resource Pack

The Workbook Resource Packs (not revised for 2011) consist of a Workbook (with or without key) and a MultiROM. The MultiROM at the back of the Workbook contains audio material linked to the Listening Sections in the Workbook. Students can play the audio in a CD player or on a computer. There is also a link which launches students to www.oxfordenglishtesting.com where they get access to two interactive online practice tests. The tests offer authentic exam practice, automatic marking for instant results and an online dictionary look-up facility. For further information, visit the website itself.

The Workbook consists of the same number of units as the Student's Book and mirrors the examination task types. The umbrella topics are the same as those in the Student's Book but the section topics are different, although they have some connection to those in the Student's Book. Each unit consists of five sections: Reading, Vocabulary, Grammar, Listening and Use of English.

Vocabulary and Grammar are given a high profile. The Vocabulary sections pick up on and extend the vocabulary introduced in the Reading texts.

Grammar both consolidates what has been taught in the Student's Book, e.g. a review of verb patterns, and introduces further mini-grammar sections in the Grammar Extra sections.

The Listening and Use of English sections give students further practice in exam task types. Please note that in the Workbook, the listening tasks are not repeated on the MultiROM as they would be in the exam.

Dictionary skills work also features in the Vocabulary and Use of English sections.

Workbook Review sections
After every three units, i.e 1–3, 4–6, 7–9, 10–12, there is a two-page review of the vocabulary and grammar in the three previous units. These enable students to check their own progress at regular intervals and identify any areas requiring further study.

Website materials

Additional materials are available on the Result Teacher's site www.oup.com/elt/teacher/result and on the Student's site at www.oup.com/elt/result .

The circle of life

Lead in p9

1 Ask students to do exercise 1 individually and to write down their answers.

2 Before students compare their answers in pairs, check they understand the physical features mentioned, especially the more difficult ones (*tanned, hazel, bushy, hooked*). Prepare examples or be ready to draw diagrams, if necessary.

3 Get the different pairs to report back their answers (and the reasons for them) to the rest of the class before checking. You could do a similar activity using photos of famous people from the students' own country, if you think the ones in the book might be unfamiliar.

Key

Scarlett Johansson (photo 1) and Hunter Johansson (photo 6) are twin sister and brother.
Ben Affleck (photo 2) and Casey Affleck (photo 7) are brothers.
Goldie Hawn (photo 3) and Kate Hudson (photo 8) are mother and daughter.
Charlie Sheen (photo 4) and Martin Sheen (photo 5) are son and father.

Background information

Scarlett Johansson is an American actress and singer; her twin brother, Hunter, is younger than her by three minutes.
Ben Affleck is an American actor, film director, writer, and producer; his younger brother, Casey, is an actor and film director.
Goldie Hawn is American actress, film director, producer, and singer; her daugher, Kate Hudson, is an actress.
Charlie Sheen is an American actor; his father, Martin Sheen, is an actor.

4 For the first two points, you might need to elicit and/or pre-teach some more vocabulary for physical descriptions: *dimples, freckles*, etc. Be careful with this activity if you suspect that any of your students might be sensitive about their physical appearance.

For the last point, personality adjectives will be covered in Vocabulary exercise 1 page 12. At this stage, just elicit and/or pre-teach a few examples, perhaps in terms of opposites, e.g. *calm/quick tempered, funny/serious, patient/impatient*, etc.

Reading p10

1 Students should discuss this in pairs or small groups. Give them a time limit of about three minutes for this warm-up discussion.

2 Give students a time limit of approximately five minutes to help them with speed reading, and encourage them not to get stuck on unknown vocabulary, as they may not need it to answer the questions.

Key

c

3 Key

1 A ✓ *By studying ... twins who have not grown up together, researchers can see ...* (l. 14–16)
  B ✗ It's already known that all identical twins have identical DNA (l. 13–14), so this is not what scientists are interested in.
  C ✗ There is no reference to this.
  D ✗ Scientists are interested in *which similarities remain* **as well as** *which disappear.* (l. 16–17).

2 A ✗ *The twins were finally reunited at age 39* (l. 46): long after they had grown up.
  B ✓ *Springer learned of his twin at age eight.* (l. 34) but had no contact with him.
  C ✗ See sentence in B above.
  D ✗ Like Jim, *his adoptive parents believed the brother had died.* (l. 35).

3 A ✗ The opposite is true: they were *amazed* by the similarities. (l. 37).
  B ✗ There is no reference to this.
  C ✗ There is no reference to this.
  D ✓ *The similarities the twins shared ... amazed one another ....* (l. 37–38). This means: 'They were both amazed by the similarities between each other.'

4 A ✗ We don't know whether this is true or not.
   B ✓ *Each Jim had been married twice.* (l. 42)
   C ✗ *As youngsters, each Jim had a dog named 'Toy'.* (l. 41).
   D ✗ There is no reference to this.
5 A ✗ Other cases are referred to as *not as eerily similar as the Jim twins.* (l. 53).
   B ✓ *While not as eerily similar as the Jim twins* (l. 53) means 'Although they are less surprising …'. The remainder of the paragraph contains examples of other interesting coincidences.
   C ✗ Other cases are referred to as *not as eerily similar as the Jim twins.* (l. 53).
   D ✗ The text does not say this.
6 A ✗ The text does not say this.
   B ✗ *This means that our character traits … are … determined before we are born.* (l. 65–66)
   C ✗ There is no reference to this.
   D ✓ *… research so far indicates that characteristics such as personality are mainly related to genes.* (l. 63–65).

Vocabulary p12

1 Ask students if any of the personality adjectives they used in the last part of exercise 4 page 9 are the same as those here. In some cases, students may not necessarily agree about which adjectives are positive or negative. Encourage them to give reasons why, with examples.

Suggested answers

a easy-going, honest, loyal, open-minded, sensible
b argumentative, arrogant, bossy, narrow-minded
c eccentric, sensitive

2 Ask students to note down the key phrases in each description. These are marked in bold in the Tapescript below. Compare answers (and key phrases) as a class.

Key

Speaker 1: narrow-minded
Speaker 2: arrogant
Speaker 3: eccentric
Speaker 4: bossy
Speaker 5: honest

Tapescript 1

Speaker 1
I don't really get on with my uncle – we disagree about almost everything! We rarely argue, though, because there's no point. **He never changes his mind!** What really annoys me is that **he won't even listen to other points of view. He doesn't realise that other people see things from other perspectives** – and might actually be able to teach him something new!

Speaker 2
I love my brother, of course, but sometimes he really annoys me. **He's always talking about how popular he is, and how good he is at sport.** I'm not saying that he isn't – I'm just saying he shouldn't talk about it! **People don't want to hear him boasting. He should learn some modesty!**

Speaker 3
It's always fun being with my friend Lulu – she's different from anyone else I know. And it's impossible to be bored when you're with her. I suppose **it's because she doesn't really care what anybody else does – she does her own thing**. For example, she wears old dresses that she buys in second-hand shops – whereas we all wear jeans and T-shirts. And the music she listens to is really unusual. **She's a bit unusual in lots of ways**, but she's good fun to be with.

Speaker 4
We go to visit our aunt and uncle in Brighton about once a month. They've got one daughter – Vanessa. She's a year younger than I am, but for some reason, **she imagines that she can tell me what to do all the time**! 'Put your coat on, we're going for a walk,' she'll say. Or if her mum asks her to wash the dishes, she tells me that I have to help! I don't argue much, because I'm such an easy-going person, but I don't really like it.

Speaker 5
My dad has got loads of friends, but he's lost a few friends over the years too, because **he's got this habit of speaking his mind**. Whatever he thinks, he says – and sometimes, people get offended. So, for example, he'll ask one of our neighbours why she's put on so much weight. He isn't exactly rude – well, he doesn't mean to be, anyway. **He's just says things as he sees them, really.**

3 Go through the **tip** box with the students and ensure that they use the modifying adverbs correctly in their descriptions.

Grammar p12

1 **Key**
   1 c   2 b   3 b   4 c   5 a   6 c   7 c

2 **Key**
   a present continuous (sentence 5)
   b *going to* future (sentence 7)
   c *will* future (sentence 3)
   d future continuous (sentence 6)
   e future perfect simple (sentence 1)

f present simple (sentence 2)

g future perfect continuous (sentence 4)

3 Encourage students to use complete sentences so you can check they use tenses correctly and consistently.

4 Check that students understand the sense of *get hold of the story* (= find out a story that is being kept hidden). Sometimes there is more than one possible answer, but students only need to give one answer for each item.

Key

Martin Hi, is Jacqui there?

Lucy Yes, she is. Wait a moment, <u>I'm just getting her</u>. *I'll just get her.*

Martin Thanks!

Jacqui Hi, it's Jacqui here.

Martin This is Martin. Listen carefully, I haven't got much time. Can you meet me at the port in one hour? The next boat to Tripoli <u>will leave</u> *leaves* (or *is leaving*) at 7.35.

Jacqui I can't! <u>I'll have</u> *I'm having* dinner with some people from work this evening. I've just arranged it.

Martin But we must leave tonight! By tomorrow morning, the newspapers <u>are going to get hold</u> *will have got hold* of the story. We <u>won't have been able</u> *won't be able* to move without attracting attention.

Jacqui What story? Are you <u>telling</u> *going to tell* me what's going on? (or *Will you tell me … ?*).

Martin <u>I explain</u> *I'll explain* everything as soon as <u>we'll get</u> *we get* to Tripoli. Trust me.

Jacqui Can't you explain now?

Martin There's no time. But if you don't do as I say, then by this time tomorrow, every journalist in town <u>will knock</u> *will be knocking* at your door.

5 Encourage students to use complete sentences when giving their reasons, so you can check they use tenses correctly and consistently.

6 Allow 10–15 minutes for the discussion. Then get the pairs to report their ideas back to the whole class.

Listening p14

1 Limit this warm-up activity to five minutes.

2 The phrases in bold in the Tapescript show where the answers can be located.

Key

1 C 2 A 3 C 4 C 5 A

Tapescript 2

P=Presenter A=Adam

P Welcome to the programme. Today, I'm joined by journalist Adam Clark, who has been researching current theories of immortality. Am I right in thinking that scientists are currently working on technology that will allow people to live for ever?

A Yes, indeed. That's exactly right. And some scientists believe that **this technology is not very far in the future – perhaps less than 30 years away – although there is still a lot of disagreement about that.** But basically, the first person to live for hundreds, possibly thousands, of years could already be alive today. Perhaps some of the people listening now will live for thousands of years. It's certainly very possible.

P What makes it possible? It's never been possible in the past, has it? Although people have often talked about it.

A I think the situation now is really different from at any time in the past. New medical and scientific techniques mean that it's becoming possible to repair the human body. **Gradually, scientists are coming to understand why our bodies deteriorate with age –** what happens to the cells in our bodies – and they're starting to find ways of stopping this. In short, they're finding ways to stop the ageing process.

P It's an exciting idea, isn't it?

A Well, yes and no! Some people actually think it's a very worrying idea – they aren't in favour of it at all.

P Why not?

A Well, **they argue that there are already too many people in the world.** Our planet is very crowded, and we're finding it difficult to feed all of them already. So imagine a situation in which people start living for hundreds of years. They'll be alive to see not only their grandchildren, but their great-great-great-great-grandchildren too. You'll have nine, ten or more generations of the same family all alive at the same time. **Population will spiral out of control!**

P And Christmas will be a nightmare!

A Absolutely. People have thought about this problem, of course. They have two main suggestions for dealing with it. Firstly, they say that we'll have to go into space and colonise other planets. And secondly, they say that people who want to live for ever will have to agree to only have one or two children. But I'm not sure that these suggestions would really solve the problem entirely.

P Are there any other disadvantages to the idea of being able to live for ever?

A Yes, perhaps. There might be a problem with **motivation. Why get up in the morning, if we know that there will be thousands of other mornings just the same?** In fact, why do anything today, if we've got a thousand years in which to do it?

P Interesting.

A Other people argue that it would be pointless to live for ever because you wouldn't be able to remember more than, say, 100 years of your past. So in a way, you wouldn't really know that you'd lived longer than that.

P Your past would be like another life.

A Yes, that's right. And there are other possible disadvantages. Some people believe that living for ever would completely change what it means to be human. They argue that **our time is only important to us** – that everything, in fact, is only important – **because we know it won't last for ever.** So if we knew we were going to live forever, we might never be able to experience the most powerful human emotions, like falling in love.

P So, in a way, if we developed technology which allowed us to become immortal, we'd stop being completely human.

A That's right. You could argue that the longer somebody lives, the less interesting life becomes for that person.

P Adam, thank you.

3 Elicit/pre-teach vocabulary for talking about different age groups before starting the discussion, e.g. *(I'd like to be ...) a teenager/in my twenties/ middle-aged*, etc.

Speaking p15

1 Key

a 4 b 1 c 5 d 2 e 6 f 3

Optional activity

Ask students to suggest more words that can be added to each of the pairs of words in 1–6. For example, extra words for 1 could include: *playing games, socialising, shopping online.*

2 Key

1 d 2 c 3 a 4 f 5 b 6 e

Tapescript 3

1 Two years ago, I went on holiday in the Italian Alps. We stayed at a resort called Cortina. The scenery was amazing. There were snow-capped mountains, pine forests, rivers and streams. I love the Alps. They're as spectacular as any mountain range in the world – in my view, anyway. Although I've never actually been to the Himalayas.

2 She's called Emma. She's got short, dark hair and green eyes. She's about the same height as me. We get on well because we're both really easy-going. She's a little bit eccentric, but as a friend, she's very loyal. That's my opinion, anyway.

3 I wouldn't say that I like being by myself all the time. I mean, it's often more fun doing things when you're with a friend, because you can share the experience and talk about it. But on the other hand, I think I need some time for solitary activities – reading or listening to music, for example. It helps me to relax. So in short, yes, I enjoy being alone, but not all the time!

4 Let me see. It's probably a series called *Lost.* I like it because the plot is really exciting and the special effects are great. In general, I like dramas more than any other kind of programme. But at the same time, I enjoy watching comedies like *The Simpsons* occasionally.

5 I mainly go online when I need to do research for schoolwork – a project, for example. I find it much quicker and easier than using reference books. Although I must admit, information on the Internet is not always reliable! I also use the Internet for downloading music. And that's about it, really.

6 That's a difficult question to answer, because I enjoy both kinds. I find it satisfying when I do well in an exam, for example. Having said that, I also really like the feeling of achievement you get from doing something like climbing a steep hill. So all in all ... I don't really know which I like more.

3 Suggest to students that they learn a selection of these 'signalling' expressions by heart, but also point out that they should try to use them appropriately and avoid over-using them.

Key

a in *(end of answer)*

b opinion *(end of answer)*

c the other *(contrast)*

d in *(end of answer)*

e same *(contrast)*

f admit *(contrast)*

g it *(end of answer)*

h that *(contrast)*

i in *(end of answer)*

4 Ask individual students to volunteer examples of questions they have written, and review them with the whole class. You may need to do some extra work on question forms, as well as on the specific vocabulary needed for each topic.

Use of English p16

1 Suggest that students start by matching the phrases they know, then use their dictionary for the others.

Key

a 5   b 2   c 6   d 1   e 4   f 3

2 This question is designed to prepare students for exercise 3, by giving them practice in turning expressions into single-verb equivalents. (They will do the reverse in exercise 3.) Other answers may be possible here, but students only need to find a single answer for each item.

Suggested answers

1 help (out)
2 forgets
3 told her
4 contacted
5 apologise
6 promised

3 All the vocabulary practised here has already been covered in exercises 1 and 2. To make this activity more challenging for stronger students, ask them to cover up the left-hand column and then uncover it to check their answers.

Key

a take part in
b to say sorry for
c take into account how
d get in touch
e make fun of
f gave (her) our word

Vocabulary p17

1 Key

a tear (meaning 'move very fast'): *The car belted down the road* = *The car tore down the road.*
   shut up (synonym of **belt up** (meaning 'stop talking')
b dark/deep
c below the belt/belt and braces/have sth under your belt/pale beside (or next to) sth/pale in (or by) comparison/pale into insignificance/beyond the pale
d belt up, meaning to fasten your seatbelt/belt up, meaning to be quiet

e buckle up (= belt up)
f belt = the act of hitting sth/belt and braces/have sth under your belt/belt = to hit/belt = to move very fast/belt sth out/belt up
g belt sth out/belt up
h belt up = shut up

2 Key

a (belt) noun 3
b (pale) adjective 1
c (pale) adjective 3
d (belt) verb 2
e (belt) noun 4
f (pale) adjective 2

3 Key

a Drivers and passengers should **belt up** even for short journeys.
b Just **belt up**! I can't hear myself think!
c His salary **pales** in comparison with the amount of money his wife earns.
d Some of the comedian's jokes were **beyond the pale**.
e The van was **belting along** the motorway at 140 kph.
f As the last song of the concert, the band **belted out** *America the Beautiful*.

Writing p18

1 Remind students that a good learner's dictionary will normally say whether a word is formal, and will also give an informal equivalent.

Suggested answers

Formal	Informal
examinations	exams
therefore	so
resides	lives
sufficient	enough
purchase	buy/get
employment	work/a job
commence	start/begin
encountered	met

2 Key

b, d, g

3 Key

Paragraph a ends with ' ... absolutely nothing!'
Paragraph b ends with ' ... to myself!'
Paragraph c ends with ' ... replace him!'
The remainder of the letter is Paragraph d.

4 Key

Formal	Informal
assist	help
informed	told
resembles	looks like
funds	money/cash

5 Key

sentence a	end of paragraph b
sentence b	end of paragraph a
sentence c	end of paragraph d
sentence d	after first or second sentence in paragraph c

Optional activity

Once students have matched the sentences to the paragraphs, you could discuss exactly where the extra sentences should go. (The most obvious place is at the end of each paragraph, except for sentence d, which could also go after '... *I'm going to look for employment/a job'*.)

6 Students might need some help with ideas. You should encourage them to adapt the categories to fit their personal experience, and/or add new categories of their own.

7 Give students an example of a paragraph plan, pointing out what information needs to be included. For example, Megan's paragraph plan for her letter might look like this:

Immediate future

- 15–21 June: A week doing nothing. (I've told friends I don't want to go out.)

A trip abroad

- Visiting my uncle in Italy (2 weeks?)
- He bought my ticket (I don't have enough money.)
- He will be working so I'll have house to myself. (House has swimming pool!)
- Just have to help with housework

Getting a job

- Need to earn money before next school year.
- Take over my brother's job at the leisure centre? (He's going to university.)

Questions for Chloe

- What are her plans for summer?
- Is she visiting the Spanish girl she met at Easter? (She looks like Penelope Cruz.)

8 When checking students' answers, pay particular attention to correct use of linking expressions and informal vocabulary.

There is an assessed authentic answer to this task on page 6 of the *Writing and Speaking Assessment Booklet*.

Review p20

1 Key

a	5		d	6
b	1		e	4
c	2		f	3

2 Key

a	starts		d	won't be playing
b	correct		e	I'm going to stand
c	I'm having/I'll be having/I'm going to have		f	Will you have left

3 Key

a	arrive		d	know
b	will lose		e	will have
c	will be		f	will help

4 Key

1	play		4	have
2	make		5	say
3	make			

5 Key

a took everybody's opinion into account
b give me your word
c got in touch with
d to take part in

Wild

Lead in p21

1 Once they have done the task, explain to students that there were two different kinds of key expressions:

(1) ones that showed whether the speakers live in the city or the countryside (mainly nouns); and (2) ones that showed whether or not they are happy with where they live (mainly verbs and adjectives). In Tapescript 4 below, type (1) key expressions are in bold, and type (2) are underlined.

Also, check that students understand the two different meanings of *used to/be used to* as used by Speakers 3 and 4.

Key

Speaker 1 lives is in a city and is happy with it.
Speaker 2 lives in the countryside and is happy with it.
Speaker 3 lives in the countryside and is not happy with it.
Speaker 4 lives in the city and is not happy with it.
Speaker 5 lives in the countryside and is happy with it.

Tapescript 4

1
I just <u>love</u> the feeling of space. The view from my bedroom window is fantastic – I can see for miles **over the rooftops**, all the way to the river in the distance. But when I go down to **street-level**, I'm right in the middle of everything, so it's <u>convenient</u> too.

2
For the kinds of hobbies we enjoy doing, this is the <u>perfect</u> place to live. The **scenery** around here is <u>amazing</u>. And **there's no need to** put the bikes on the back of the car and **drive for ages just to find an open road – we just go out of the front door** and set off. I'd feel trapped if I couldn't do that.

3
I've been here for nearly a year now. I **used to live in London** and I moved here because property prices are so much lower – but <u>it's not for me. I feel so isolated here!</u> I mean, my next-door neighbour is five kilometres away. **There are no facilities nearby – you have to get in the car** and drive somewhere else even if you just want a loaf of bread.

4
I grew up in a village, so I'm used to knowing my neighbours. <u>It's weird living here.</u> **There are two hundred people living in this building**, and I don't know any of them! Most of them don't even say hello when you get into the lift with them. There's no sense of community. <u>That's why I don't like it.</u> When I was a boy, we didn't even lock our front door. Now I'm nervous every time I open it.

5
<u>I love</u> **the peace and quiet**. Before I moved here, I was so stressed the whole time – I never stopped to listen to the birds, or look at the horizon. But now I do. **It's a slower pace of life**, and <u>that suits me really well</u>. **The air is cleaner, too** – fewer busy roads means less pollution.

2 Get students to compare answers in pairs, using a dictionary if necessary.

Key

a view
b right
c scenery
d isolated
e facilities
f community
g quiet

3 Encourage students to compare the photos as in Paper 5 Part 2. The first two points in the **how to do it** box on page 123 may be useful. Check that they understand all the adjectives provided, and which are normally used for the city and which for the countryside, and get them to add others of their own.

4 Remind students to use a range of the liking and disliking expressions in the listening activity, and not just to say *I like* and *I don't like*.

Reading p22

1 Check that students understand *herd*, *roots*, *herbivore*, *palms*, *shepherd* before answering.

Key

a all of them
b antelope
c monkey
d antelope (and possibly monkey, though some may eat meat)
e monkey
f dog

2 Tell students that they need to scan the text to find this information. The exercise is harder than it looks, especially because the children's ages at the time they were found are not always given directly, but sometimes need to be inferred (see Key). This highlights the importance of reading each question carefully in the exam.

Key

a

A in a forest in Uganda

B the Spanish Sahara

C the North Cachar Hills in India

D in a cardboard box in a forest in Romania

b

A five or six: i.e. he was found in 1991 and was three years older than when he was last seen in 1988 *at the age of two or three*. (l. 10)

B about 10 (l. 24)

C five: *who was now five* means 'who was five at the time he was found'. (l. 45)

D about seven: he was *lost three years earlier at the age of four.* (l. 67–68). (Also check that they've understood that *actual age* (l. 64) means 'real age'.)

3 The most obvious way to label the four sections is probably by the relevant animal, i.e.

A monkey boy

B gazelle boy

C leopard boy

D dog boy

Adding headings may help students to remember which paragraph they have read key information in.

Key

1 B (l. 33–34)

2 D (l. 63–65)

3 A (l. 11–13)

4 B (l. 25)

5 D (l. 70–71) B is ruled out as a possible answer (l. 37–39): see question 9 below.

6 C (l. 47–48)

7 D (l. 65–66)

8 A (l. 15)

9 B (l. 37–39)

10 C (l. 50–51)

11 A (l. 14)

12 C (l. 44–45) The children in A and D were not taken by a wild animal, but were lost.

13 B (l. 30–31). Refer students back to exercise 1 d, explaining that *herbivorous* is the adjective and *herbivore* is the noun.

14 B (l. 27–28).

15 A (l. 16–18).

4 See if students are able to match any of the phrasal vebs before they refer back to the text. They can then use the context provided in the text to confirm their answers.

Key

a 4   b 1   c 5   d 2   e 6   f 3

5 Get students to prepare in pairs, making notes under each of the headings. Then have a whole-class discussion.

Encourage students to use appropriate verb structures as part of the discussion, e.g.

*They **would/might find it hard** to eat normal food.*

*They **will have missed** a lot of education.*

*They **won't be able to** make friends easily.*

Vocabulary p24

1 Students can discuss the photos in pairs or as a class. If they do this in pairs, get them to make a note of any vocabulary they have problems with, and review it with the rest of the class.

2 Students may know the difference between the words but find it difficult to explain in English. If you have a monolingual class, you could allow them to try to explain the difference in their own language before they refer to their dictionary.

Key

a   **valley** (the only one which is a lower area of ground, not a raised area)

A **mountain** is taller and often rockier than a **hill**. A **dune** is a hill of sand.

b   **desert** (the only one which is not a body of water – a desert is a large, inhospitable area without much vegetation)

A **lake** is larger than a **pond**. **Ponds** are often man-made and found in gardens and parks, whereas lakes are usually natural. A **lagoon** is an area of the sea which is separated by a long, thin piece of land or a coral reef, forming a kind of lake.

c   **field** (the only one which is not an area of trees – a field is a cultivated area of grass or crops)

A **forest** covers a larger area than a **wood**. A **jungle** contains very dense vegetation and is usually found near the equator in regions with a very wet climate.

d **plain** (the only one not related to the sea or water – a plain is a large, flat area of land)

A **beach** is a thin strip of sandy or stony land bordering the sea. **Shore** is another word for beach, but can also refer to the land around the edge of a lake or other large body of water. **Coast** is a more general term for the area of land near the sea.

e **waterfall** (the only one not related to vegetation – a waterfall is a steep drop in the level of a river or stream)

A **bush** is a plant with woody branches and leaves, but unlike a tree, it has no trunk. A **hedge** is a border or fence created by planting bushes close together in a line.

3 Suggested answers

1   mountain, beach, shore, coast, bush
2   plain, tree
3   dune, desert
4   valley, hill, field, wood, hedge

Grammar p25

1 Key

Imagine finding
hope to be rescued
risk getting
spend time searching
postpone worrying
managed to find or build a shelter
keep reading

2 Show students how they can use their dictionary to find out whether a verb is followed by an infinitive, an -ing form or both and explain that they should note which whenever they learn a new verb.

Key

Group A imagine, risk, spend time, postpone, keep
Group B hope, manage

3 Key

1 making
2 enlarging
3 to be
4 to build (Explain that the verb *stop* can be followed by both forms, but that each has a different meaning. *Stop to build* means 'stop

moving and build your shelter'. *Stop building* would mean 'don't build your shelter any more'.)

5 to find
6 walking (Explain that *try walking* is used for suggestions, and means 'One thing you could do is …'. *Try to walk* would mean that the writer thought that walking would be difficult for some reason.)

7 drinking
8 eating (Make sure that they understand *If you can't face …* meaning 'to be unable or unwilling to deal with something unpleasant'.)

9 to approach
10 looking (Check that they know that *give up* means 'abandon' here.)

11 eating
12 doing

4 Point out that both a and b forms are possible, but that the meaning is different. You can demonstrate this by showing an alternative context for the option they don't select. e.g. question 3: *He tried **to open** the window. **But it was completely stuck.***

Key

1 b   2 a   3 b   4 a

5 Suggested answers

a   … **to study** at university./… **seeing** my old friends.
b   … **to let** other people pass./… **ignoring** me.
c   … **to give up** smoking./**cycling** to college instead of driving.
d   … **to send** my mother a card on her birthday./… **going** on a plane for the first time.

Listening p26

1 Tell students to speed read the text and explain the meaning in a single sentence.

Suggested answer

Wilderness therapy is a way of helping young people who have problems, by sending them on a survival course in a remote area.

2 Tell students to justify their answers by referring to specific phrases. For example, Rachael's comment: *'you might as well make it a positive experience, rather than being negative'*. And Rachael's mother: *'I think Utah and RedCliff have worked magic.'* Ed's experience was less positive; this comes at the end: (*'For Ed, the RedCliff has not been such a success story … its benefits were short-lived.'*)

Key

Rachael

Tapescript 5

Presenter Some people call it 'Brat Camp' – because many of the young people who go there have, at some time or other, **been in trouble with the law**. All of them have personal or social problems which RedCliff Ascent in Utah, USA, aims to resolve through what is known as 'Wilderness therapy'. Many of the teenagers who attend the programmes at RedCliff **are almost impossible to control – and their parents are out of ideas**. One teenage boy who recently completed the programme was described as 'abusive, arrogant, foul-mouthed and ill-disciplined' – and that was by his mother. In this programme we meet two of these teenagers, and find out how successful the camp has been for them. Rachael was happy at school with lots of friends and **was very good at long-distance running**. She was even enjoying being in the police cadets. But everything seemed to change when she became a Goth. She was told to leave the cadets for failing to remove the 18 earrings, nose rings and other piercings she wore, and she began staying out all night, never letting her mum know where she was. Immediately after her time at RedCliff Ascent, Rachael returned to England and decided she wanted to **plan a career working with animals**. One year after the camp, Rachael is studying for a course in animal management in a top North London college. As part of her studies she is planning a study trip working with animals abroad this year. **Things are still good between Rachael and her mum**. This is how Rachael describes the change.

Rachael You can look at me and say, you know, she hasn't changed, but inside I feel like I'm a completely different person now. You just realise that you're at RedCliff and you might as well make it a positive experience, rather than being negative all the time about it.

Presenter Helen, Rachael's mum, is even more positive.

Helen **She looks beautiful**, really beautiful. There's a glow to her face that brings tears to my eyes. That was what Rachael was like two or three years before, and now she's back to being that Rachael. I think Utah and RedCliff have worked magic.

Presenter Another teenager who was sent to RedCliff is Ed. The situation for Ed and his family was terrible. Ed has an older brother and sister. He has always argued with them and has stolen from them both, as well as stealing a laptop computer from his mother, Jane. On two occasions he had to be found and brought home by the police. To stop his family falling apart **he had to move out and find a new home**. Ed's mother, Jane, did not know what she could do to help him.

Jane When Ed was born my mum looked into the cot and said, 'That one is going to be an archbishop or an arch criminal.' He can be really lovely to his brother and sister and then walk out with their CDs and mobile phones. **However much money you make available to him it's never going to be enough.'** When I threw him out I told him, 'I've got to throw you out, you are not living here any more. The fact that I am doing this shows you how desperate I am.' I've got a comfortable home and I've failed, I've failed my son and he is going to end up in the gutter. That's how desperate I am. To admit all that is pretty horrible.

Presenter For Ed, the RedCliff has not been such a success story. He attended the programme there, but its benefits were short-lived. He went back to his old ways more or less as soon as he got back to England.

Jane The camp made some difference at first, but **Ed started stealing again after just two weeks at home**. He has low self-esteem and he has made a poor choice of friends.

Presenter But despite these setbacks, Jane has not given up hope. Recently, Ed went back to the camp in Utah for a further course of therapy. **His mother hopes that this time it will prove more successful**. In many ways, she regards it as Ed's last chance.

3 The phrases in bold in the Tapescript show where the answers can be located.

Key

1	law	6	beautiful
2	control	7	home
3	running	8	money
4	animals	9	stealing
5	mother	10	successful

4 Encourage students to use vocabulary and structures from this section in their discussion. Focus on key expressions such as *it helps them to…* ; *they learn how to …* ; *it stops them from … -ing*, which you can also use to revise the topic of infinitive and *-ing* structures after verbs that is covered in the **Grammar** section of this unit.

Speaking p27

1 Get students to look ahead to the **how to do it** box for describing photos on page 123.

Check that they understand the more difficult expressions used in the sentences, e.g. *a remote landscape, dense vegetation, snow-capped mountains.*

Key

a   photo 2 (and probably 1)

b   photo 2

c   photo 1

d   photo 2

e   photo 2

f   photo 2

Optional activity

Find out if students have visited places with similar landscapes or can suggest countries where such landscapes might be found.

2   Check that students understand *in single file* and *side by side*.

Suggested answers

a   The people in photo 1 are walking through the jungle.

b   The people in photo 2 are in the middle of a mountain range.

c   The people in photo 2 are (travelling) on/riding mountain bikes.

d   The people in photo 1 are exploring on foot.

e   The people in photo 1 are walking in single file.

f   The people in photo 2 are cycling side by side.

g   The people in photo 2 are wearing long-sleeved jackets.

h   The people in photo 1 are wearing short-sleeved T-shirts.

i   The people in in photo 2 are surrounded by spectacular scenery.

j   The people in photo 1 are surrounded by dense vegetation.

3   Suggested answers

Speaker 1 is talking about photo 2. Key words could include: *steep, drop, heights.*

Speaker 2 is talking about photo 2. Key words could include: *top, climbing, high.*

Speaker 3 is talking about photo 1. Key words could include: *gloomy, branches, leaves.*

Speaker 4 is talking about photo 2. Key words could include: *excited, mountain range, Himalayas, top, spectacular, views.*

Speaker 5 is talking about photo 1. Key words could include: *humid, jungle, insect.*

Tapescript 6

Speaker 1

I think the people could be feeling quite nervous, because it looks as though they're really near the edge. It's probably a very steep drop. Personally, I would be terrified in their situation, because I've got a phobia about heights.

Speaker 2

I imagine that they might be feeling quite tired. It looks as if they've reached the top, more or less, so we can assume that they've already covered a lot of distance. At the same time, they must be feeling really pleased with themselves for having reached the top. I love that sense of achievement you get from climbing up really high.

Speaker 3

It looks as if they're quite bored. They aren't looking around, just at the person in front. That's because they can't see very much. It's very gloomy, and there are too many branches and leaves in the way. I don't think I'd enjoy this kind of trek. I hate the idea of not being able to see very far ahead!

Speaker 4

They must be feeling excited. It looks like a huge mountain range – possibly the Himalayas – so they must feel as though they're on top of the world! I'd imagine the air to be really fresh and clean. I'd feel really excited in that situation. I've always loved mountains and spectacular views.

Speaker 5

They're probably feeling a bit hot and sweaty, because it's usually very humid in the jungle. I expect they're itching from all the insect bites too! I would hate being in that kind of climate. I'd feel as though I couldn't breathe.

4   When they have finished, focus on examples of hypothesising language, e.g. *I think the people could be …; … it looks as though …; It's probably …,* etc. (This is something students need to be able to do in Paper 5 Part 2, where they will get credit for speculating about the photos.)

Also, point out the use of *would* by the speaker: *Personally, I **would** be …; I don't think I'd enjoy* … . Finally, when checking the answer for g, you could mention that when *must* is used in hypothesising, it's normally stressed in speech: (*They **must** be feeling exhilarated.*)

Key

a	nervous	e	if
b	terrified	f	idea
c	imagine	g	must
d	sense	h	probably

5   Students can discuss these points in pairs or small groups. Ask them to take turns in asking and answering the questions.

Use of English p28

1 Draw students' attention to the **tip** box before beginning the activity. Encourage them to try to answer all the questions before they look at their dictionaries.

Key

1	a to	b	on
2	a in	b	at
3	a of	b	with
4	a for	b	of
5	a in	b	of
6	a of	b	about

2 **Key**

a	at	f	by
b	on	g	on
c	in	h	at
d	on	i	over
e	to		

3 Tell students to answer the question using no more than two sentences.

Suggested answer

Some people think Cute Knut should have been allowed to die because raising him by hand is so unnatural. In the wild, he would have died.

4 Tell students there may occasionally be more than one possible alternative (although they only need to find one word). Also remind them that not all the missing words will be prepositions.

Key

1	all	7	of
2	with	8	too
3	in	9	have
4	would	10	he
5	by	11	as
6	with (*or* among)	12	with (*or* in)

5 The discussion can be done either in pairs or as a class, depending on how much time is available.

Vocabulary p29

1 Get students to work in pairs and encourage them to do as much as they can before consulting their dictionaries.

Key

a birds, sheep
b cows, elephants
c cards, dogs
d bananas, flowers

Optional activity

Tell students to add one or two other nouns to each list, e.g. b *goats, cattle* d *grapes*. Elicit other collective nouns. You could also tell them to use *a set of* for groups of items that need a fixed number to be complete, e.g. *dishes, cutlery, tyres*, etc.

2 Point out that, in writing or speaking activities, students can use the expressions in 1–8 (*people who … ; a group of people who …*) when they don't know – or can't remember – the correct collective noun.

Key

a 4
b 1
c 7 (A *film crew* or *TV crew* are the people working on the productions who are not actors, e.g. lighting and sound engineers, camera operators, etc.)
d 6
e 8
f 5
g 3
h 2

3 **Key**

a	gangs	e	cast
b	flock	f	bunch
c	herd	g	crowd
d	staff	h	audience

Writing p30

1 Remind students that this is a formal email so their answers should rephrase the language into a less formal style.

Suggested answer

How long are volunteers expected to stay in Peru? How physically challenging is the expedition?

2 Remind students that they will normally be able to find less formal equivalents in a good learner's dictionary.

Suggested answers

a asking for
b happening soon
c have
d managed to get
e idea
f difficulty
g answer

3 **Key**

a 4 request = ask for : further = more
b 2 most = very : respond to = answer; queries = questions; swiftly = quickly
c 5 prompt = fast
d 1 hearing = getting a reply
e 3 further to = following : clarify = make clear; require = need

4 Remind students that in Paper 2 Part 1 they need to use grammatically correct sentences with accurate punctuation in a style appropriate to the situation. Elicit that the style of the email is fairly formal (point to the use of formal words in the text such as: *therefore*, *is desirable*, *is required*); so, a formal style of response is appropriate here.

There is an assessed authentic answer to this task on page 7 of the *Writing and Speaking Assessment Booklet*.

Review p32

1 **Key**

a waterfall, valley
b lagoon, jungle
c coast, beaches
d dunes, desert
e pond, bushes

2 **Key**

a smoking
b relaxing
c to study
d seeing
e going
f eating
g to arrive
h walking

3 **Key**

a to do
b playing
c tapping
d to move
e to tie
f talking

4 **Key**

1 on
2 of
3 about
4 at
5 on

What's so funny? 3

Lead in p33

1 Key

a amusing comical funny hilarious humorous hysterical

b bizarre mysterious funny unusual peculiar odd strange weird

Funny belongs in both groups.

Reading p34

1 Encourage students to describe the photos and to speculate about the abilities the two men have. Compare answers as a class before students check their ideas in 2.

2 Mr Magnet (Liew Thow Lin), shown on page 34, can 'stick' metal objects to his skin. Monsieur Mangetout (Michel Lotito), shown on page 35, can eat objects made from metal, glass, rubber, and plastic. Hai Ngoc hasn't slept since 1973. Ben Underwood was blind but could find his way around using a form of sonar.

3 Key

1 H The sentence explains what Mr Lin does as an entertainer. The words *now* and *recently* also show a connection. The sentence after the gap gives more information about what he did.

2 E The word *curious* relates back to the magazine article which he read, and which made him try sticking the metal objects to himself.

3 F The phrase *on the contrary* shows a contrast with the evil plans of Gustav Graves; Hai Ngoc uses his time positively and an example of this is given after the gap.

4 B The phrase *In fact* shows a contrast between the idea that his health may be damaged and the fact that he is physically strong. This also contrasts with *however* after the gap.

5 A *The answer* refers to the question before the gap. The sentence after the gap explains how Ben used sound to navigate.

6 G *However* and *sixteen* show a contrast with *when he was a child*.

7 C The word *also* shows something in addition to *stomach acids*; *go down* shows a connection with *digest*, and *all* shows a connection with *some of the metal*. *Water and oil* contrast with *surprisingly, bananas and eggs*.

4 Key

See the references in the key to exercise 3.

Vocabulary p36

1 Get students to answer as many as they can, then check their answers in pairs.

Key

a gorgeous	g astounded
b hideous	h hilarious
c filthy	i furious
d spotless	j exhausted
e boiling	k ancient
f freezing	l starving

2 You could show students how to use a thesaurus. Explain that some of these synonyms are less commonly used than others and that they should try to learn them in context.

Suggested answers

a huge, enormous, massive, giant, vast, gigantic, mammoth

b tiny, minute, miniature, microscopic

c great, fantastic, fabulous, amazing, excellent, incredible, wonderful, superb, super, brilliant

d awful, terrible, dreadful, appalling

3 Explain that this activity depends on recognising two kinds of adverbs or adjectives. One group (*totally, completely, absolutely, utterly*) is used when you want to say that something is **totally** the way you're describing it. The other group (*extremely, rather, quite, a bit*) is used when you want to describe **how much** something is the way you're describing it.

Spotless means 'as clean as you can get'. So a cooker can't be *a bit spotless* or *very spotless*. On the other hand, a train can't be *completely, utterly,* or *totally late*; instead, you need to say **how** late it was.

Key

a	totally	d	quite
b	extremely	e	very
c	absolutely		

Grammar p36

1 Key

a *I've been doing* (incomplete action)

b *hadn't arrived* (an event which took place before another event in the past)

c *I've had* (an experience at a non-specific time in the past)

d *found* (a short action which interrupts a longer action)

e *had been running* (explaining a situation in the past)

f *ridden* (used after 'Have you ever …?' to refer to an experience at a non-specific time in the past)

g *had closed* (used after 'When…', 'By the time …', etc. to refer to an event which took place before another event in the past)

h *wasn't wearing* (a background event)

2 Explain to students that some verbs are not used with continuous tenses and then refer them to the list of non-continuous verbs in the Grammar Reference (see p.164).

Key

a I've never believed in Santa Claus.

b I've asked him three times …

c Rita and Ahmed arrived two minutes ago.

d … the fire had been burning for over an hour.

e How long have you been studying Chinese?

f … the thieves left the country …

g How often have you travelled by plane?

h … my uncle arrived last night.

3 Check answers with the whole class. Write the students' different answers to the same question on the board, pointing out how more than one tense can sometimes be appropriate.

Suggested answers

a … I'd like to try.

b … she had been swimming.

c … it started raining.

d … it had closed.

e … have been working …

f … has been on holiday …

g … got into the car.

h … was still wide awake.

4 Suggested answers

1 had gone

2 was sitting

3 had been crying

4 've been waiting

5 've phoned

6 hasn't come

7 offered

8 accepted

9 were walking ('walked' is equally acceptable)

10 touched

11 've been thinking

12 've met

5 Tell students you will be giving credit for good use of vocabulary, spelling, punctuation, etc. as well as for correct use of tenses. When you have marked the stories, go through some of them in class as a way of revising this topic. You could also offer a prize for the most original/entertaining story.

Listening p38

1 This exercise is intended to encourage students to read the exam task carefully, and to think about the situations they are going to hear. Trying to predict the type of vocabulary they might hear for each one is good preparation for the task, especially as the situations are unconnected.

2 **Key**

a   3
b   5
c   7
d   2
e   1
f   6
g   4

Tapescript 7

1
It started on 30th January 1962 when three girls in a boarding school in Tanzania began laughing – and couldn't stop. The symptom spread to other students, although apparently the teachers were not affected. Eventually, the school had to close and the students went home. But that wasn't the end of it. **The epidemic spread to one of the villages that the girls went home to – and from there, to other schools and villages in the region.** People affected by the epidemic suffered from frequent attacks of laughter which made them unable to work or study.

2
For a start, I asked for a room with a sea view. This one overlooks the street. But I could live with that if the room itself wasn't such a disaster. The TV doesn't work. The alarm clock is broken too. Not that I could *sleep*, of course – not in that **hard, lumpy old** bed. I even tried the armchair instead, but that was no better. You know, **I wouldn't have cared about the TV or the clock – if only I'd been able to sleep!**

3
Interviewer Steve. How's it going in there?
Steve Fine. I've been training for months, but nothing can prepare you for the real thing.
Interviewer How do you train for something like this?
Steve Well, a lot of it's mental. Spending hours in such a small space can do strange things to your mind!
Interviewer So how do you prevent that?
Steve I've been learning to meditate – and trying to relax.
Interviewer It must be hard to relax with 200 snakes in the box.
Steve It doesn't help! But **I'm not giving up now.**
Interviewer You've got 24 hours to go. Can you make it?
Steve I'm sure I can.

4
Yes, I heard you lost your job, Martin. I was sorry to hear that. Really sorry. But you're still young. What, thirty-one? You've got good qualifications and excellent people skills. **I'm sure you won't have any problem finding something else.** And anyway, you didn't like your job, did you? Hang on – look, sorry, Martin. I've got a call waiting – I think it's important. Can I call you back later? Actually, why don't I call you this evening? OK – must go. But look, **don't let this get you down, will you?** OK. Bye.

5
Really exciting, it was. Best holiday ever. We travelled most of the way by coach – it took us over 24 hours. We didn't stop for the night, just slept in our seats. That wasn't very comfortable! Then it was an exhausting three-day walk through the heat of the jungle. We all had backpacks with tents in them – spent two nights sleeping in the jungle! **It was terrifying** – all those weird noises at night. **But fascinating too. And waking up in the jungle is amazing** …

6
The most important thing is to work out what people really want – because they often don't know. They *think* they know. But they haven't really considered all the angles. For example, **one couple asked me to come up with a new house** for them in the country. We talked about what kind of property they wanted and **I suggested a few ideas for what it could look like.** But as we talked about it, it became clear that they *hated* the countryside! What they should have done is just buy an apartment in central London, not build a house in the middle of nowhere!

7
Jo-Anne Bachorowski of Vanderbilt University asked 97 volunteers to watch various film extracts, and secretly taped their laughter. This left the researchers with more than a thousand bursts of laughter to analyse. 'One of the biggest surprises was the variety of sounds that constitute laughter,' she says. Laughter can be 'voiced' or song-like, such as giggles and chuckles, or unvoiced, like grunts and snorts. Most of the subjects produced a wide range of laughter types. But **women produce voiced, song-like bursts of laughter more often than men**, Bachorowski found, while **men are more likely to grunt and snort.**

3 The phrases in bold in the Tapescript show where the answers can be located.

Key

1   B
2   C
3   A
4   B
5   A
6   C
7   B

Speaking p39

1 Key

Photo 1 is modern dance. Photo 2 is an entertainer/performer who eats lightbulbs, and probably other objects, and may do other tricks. Photo 3 is a fashion show. Photo 4 is a photography exhibition.

2 Key

The photos are mentioned in this order: photo 1 contemporary dance 'The Impossibility of Being'; photo 4 photography exhibition 'Photo Dreams'; photo 3 fashion show; photo 2 novelty act.

You could ask students what kind of show is mentioned in the tapescript but is not shown in the photos – modern sculpture made out of rubbish.

Tapescript 8

Man Do you fancy going to see something in town?

Woman Sure! Great idea! What's on?

Man I've got the paper here. I'll have a look. There's a contemporary dance performance called 'The Impossibility of Being'. I love dance, don't you? Especially modern dance.

Woman I don't find modern dance very interesting. I never have.

Man Oh, OK. Well, let's forget that then. I know. What about this – 'Photo Dreams'. It's an exhibition of weird and unusual photos. I read a review of it in a magazine. It's supposed to be brilliant. Shall we go and see that?

Woman I'm not really into photography. Is there anything else on?

Man Sure. There's an art exhibition.

Woman What kind of art?

Man It's modern sculpture – really clever. It's all made out of rubbish.

Woman Oh, right. Modern sculpture isn't my favourite kind of art. In fact, I really don't like sculpture at all.

Man No problem. There are lots of other things on. For example, there are a few tickets available for the final day of fashion week. Do you like fashion shows?

Woman To be honest, most modern fashion just makes me laugh!

Man Fine. Let's forget that, then. How about a talent show?

Woman I'm not sure. Pop music isn't really my thing.

Man It isn't just pop music. There are comedians, dancers – and novelty acts. Like this guy in the photo who eats light bulbs and keys and things like that.

Woman I'm not a big fan of novelty acts. But I suppose I could give it a go …

Man Great! Well, why don't we go to that? I'll phone up and see if they've got any tickets left.

Woman All right.

3 Key

Phrases h, f, d and b are heard, in that order.

4 Key

a find
b supposed
c into
d fact
e honest
f thing
g big

5

Encourage students to use some of the expressions from exercises 3 and 4.

Use of English p40

1

Students can discuss this in pairs or as a whole class. Allow about five minutes.

2

Check that students understand the term *sibling* (= a brother or sister). The answer to the question can be found in the first sentence of the report, but students should read the whole text to check their answer.

Key

c

3

Remind students that clues to the answers might be before or after the gap.

Key

1 B

2 A

3 A *only children* have no brothers or sisters.

4 D

5 A

6 C

7 C

8 B Remind students that *to go on to do something* means 'to do something in later life' (**not** 'to continue to do something').

9 D *findings* = 'the things you find out' (from a scientific study).

10 B

11 A

12 C *tends to* = 'is likely to'

Optional activity

You could follow this up with a brief discussion (based on students' personal experience) of what it's like being an only/youngest/oldest/middle child, and how this has affected them.

Vocabulary p41

1 If students are having difficulty, refer them to exercise 2 as the meanings may help.

Key

a up with
b down
c up
d down to
e down
f up
g up
h up to

2 Explain that the alternative words are correct, but normally sound more formal than the phrasal verbs. (An exception is c, where *accommodate* sounds unnaturally formal in this context and the normal choice would be *put me up* (as here) or *give me a room*, *let me stay*, etc.)

Key

a I must find a new apartment. I can't **tolerate** my noisy neighbours any longer!
b It's not surprising she lacks confidence. Her older siblings are always **humiliating** her.
c I couldn't find a hotel room, so my friend agreed to **accommodate** me for the night.
d He was finding it difficult to sleep at night. At first, he **explained** this as being the result of stress.
e Armed rebels tried to overthrow the government, but the army soon **suppressed** the revolt.
f I need several thousand euros to pay for a year abroad before university. Fortunately, my parents have agree to **provide** half the amount.
g Because of a shortage of oil and gas, energy companies have **increased** their prices.
h He admitted vandalising the bus stop, but claimed his friends had **persuaded** him to do it.

3 You could use this activity to anticipate some of the phrasal verbs covered in exercise 4.

4 Key

a in
b across
c out
d on
e through
f forward
g away/back
h off

Writing p42

2 Check that students know what reported speech is before they do this. Refer them to the Grammar Reference (p.168) for further information.

Suggested answers

a My dad replied that we hadn't made a decision. 'We haven't made a decision.'
b 'Are you going to buy my house?' he asked. He asked (us) if we were going to buy his house.

3 Students may know the difference between the words but find it difficult to explain in English. If you have a monolingual class, you could let them explain the difference in their own language before they refer to their dictionary.

Suggested answers

a When you **explain** something, you make it clear. When you **admit** something, you agree that it is true, but unwillingly.
b When you **remark** on something, you often do so spontaneously. When you **state** something, you say it clearly and carefully.
c When you **warn** somebody, you tell them about a danger. When you **advise** somebody, you say what you think they should do.
d To **reply** means to answer. To **add** means to say something extra.
e To **promise** means to say that you will definitely do something. To **claim** means to say that something is true, even if other people do not believe it.

The story contains *replied*, *promised* and *explained*.

4 Refer students to the table of tense changes in the section on reported speech in the Grammar Reference (see p.168).

Suggested answers

a Sarah claimed that she'd seen a UFO.

b Tom promised that he would always be a loyal friend.

c Beth warned that the alarm would go off if they opened the door.

d Denis added that it was much too late to go out.

e Claire explained that her clothes were dirty because she'd been cleaning her bike.

5 Key

1 happened

2 was sitting

3 had been playing

4 was just finishing

5 had parked

6 had

6 Get students to read the **tip** box before they do this exercise.

Key

a The last sentence could be changed to: '*I have a parcel for you,*' he said.

b very funny = hilarious; very good = great, brilliant, etc. (See Vocabulary 2c.); very tired = exhausted; very big = enormous, huge, massive, etc. (See Vocabulary 2a.)

7 Ask students to make sure they follow all the tips in their story. Remind them that the second tip, about using appropriate reporting verbs and not just *said*, was covered in exercise 3.

There is an assessed authentic answer to this task on page 8 of the *Writing and Speaking Assessment Booklet*.

Review p44

1 Suggested answers

very dirty = filthy

very clean = spotless

very tired = exhausted

very surprised = amazed

very attractive = gorgeous

very hungry = starving

very bad = dreadful

very small = tiny

2 Key

1	b	4	b
2	a	5	b
3	a		

3 Key

a put me off

b putting me down

c put up

d Put away

e put across

f putting it on

g put in

h put you up

4 Key

1	C	7	A
2	C	8	D
3	B	9	C
4	B	10	B
5	C	11	C
6	A	12	A

Inspired

Lead in p45

1 This can be a whole-class discussion. Pre-teach or elicit some relevant adjectives, e.g. *talented, energetic, creative, physically fit*, etc. as well as some of the specific language in the Suggested answers below. Elicit or explain the difference between *talent* (which you are born with) and *skill* (which you can learn and develop).

Suggested answers

Singer-songwriter:

a ability to play musical instruments and read music, a good voice, artistic creativity and imagination

b listening to music, artistic talent

c learning to sing and play a musical instrument, practising and rehearsing, trying out lots of ideas for songs

Author:

a ability to express themselves clearly, possibly to write imaginatively, use language well and accurately

b reading other books and sources of information, talking to people, travelling, news stories

c probably many hours a day of writing over many months, re-reading, checking and improving what they have written

Inventor/scientist:

a academic ability, especially in maths and science, ability to visualise objects in three dimensions, imagination

b frustration at not having the right tool for a particular job, the example of other great inventors

c probably years of academic study, lots of trial and error

Film director:

a artistic creativity and imagination, visual ability, leadership and motivational skills, ability to work in a team

b watching films, artistic talent

c long days spent filming short scenes, having to organise lots of other people

2 Students can discuss this in pairs and then report back to the class. See which are the most popular choices for each category.

Suggested answers:

artist, designer, composer, musician, conductor, writer (e.g. poet, novelist), journalist, photographer, publisher, etc.

Reading p46

1 Key

a *Franz Ferdinand* and David Gray

b *Franz Ferdinand*: Albums: *Franz Ferdinand, You could have it so much better;* Songs: *Take me out, The dark of the matinée, Michael, Do you want to, Walk away,* etc.

David Gray: Albums: *Foundling, Draw the line, White Ladder, A new day at midnight, Life in slow motion, Sell, sell, sell;* Songs: *Fugitive, Babylon, This year's love, Sail away, The other side, Be mine, The one I love,* etc.

3 Before looking at the text, ask students to read the **how to do it** box for *Gapped texts* on page 94. Encourage them to follow the stages when approaching this task. They should specifically be looking out for conjunctions that either follow on from (e.g. *at the same time, similarly, also*) or contrast with (*but, however, nevertheless*, etc.) the previous sentence.

Key

1 C This develops the idea of 'the first time you a bicycle or ride a car' in the previous sentence.

2 F This links the sentences before and after, in which Alex explains how it doesn't matter to him where he writes his songs.

3 A *it* in sentence A refers to 'a story you've never heard before'. The idea of 'los[ing] your sense of where you are' is developed in the following sentence.

4 G *But* at the beginning of sentence G suggests that the idea of when 'a song just seems to come out of nowhere' is being contrasted with having to work on turning ideas into songs The idea of a song coming from nowhere is developed in the sentence immediately after the gap.

5 H The metaphor of 'open[ing] a door in your brain' refers to the role of the unconscious mind. This follows on from the sentence before ('you shut down conscious thought') and links with the following one.

6 E This contrasts with the sentence before. Taken together, the sentences mean: 'not all songs you're inspired to write are good, **but** you know when they are good, because they are so moving.' The idea of emotions is continued in the following sentence.

7 B The reference to 'not (being) a particularly easy person to live with' is developed in the following sentence: 'I find it really hard to get back into normal life.'

The extra sentence is D.

4 a 3 b 7 c 1 d 6 e 4 f 5 g 2

5 Explain to students that in a **separable** phrasal verb, the object can go either between the verb and the particle or after the particle, e.g. *She tore the letter up* OR *She tore up the letter.*). Phrasal verbs where you can't do this are called **inseparable** (e.g. *I ran into Joe yesterday* but not ~~I ran Joe into yesterday.~~)

Key

By the use of this symbol between the object and the particle: $\longleftrightarrow$

6 Key

pick up (separable), turn into (inseparable), shut down (separable), think up (separable), start off (separable)

Vocabulary p48

1 Get students to answer individually, then compare answers as a class. Encourage them to include locally produced films as well. There might be some interesting discussion if they can't agree which category a specific film falls into.

2 a funny, gripping, powerful
b boring, slow, terrible
c moving, scary, serious, violent

3 If you have limited time, choose two or three of the film types and have a class discussion.

4 Ask each pair to report back on any disagreements. Get them to note down relevant vocabulary not included in exercise 2.

Grammar p48

1 Key

a past continuous/<u>past simple</u> *had dinner*
b present continuous/<u>present simple</u> *tastes*
c <u>past continuous</u>/past simple *was rising*
d <u>present continuous</u>/present simple *are playing*
e <u>present perfect continuous</u>/ present perfect simple *Have you been sitting*
f present perfect continuous/ <u>present perfect simple</u> *has played*
g <u>future continuous</u>/future simple *'ll be sitting*
h present continuous/<u>present simple</u> *don't believe*
i <u>present perfect continuous</u>/ present perfect simple *'ve been walking*
j future continuous/<u>future simple</u> *'ll regret*
k present simple/<u>present continuous</u> *'m always leaving*

2 Key

a you have
b I remember, stood
c I remember
d don't understand
e sleep, seem

Optional activity

Get students to find other quotations of their own, either by looking at a dictionary of quotations or by translating well-known quotations or sayings from their own language. They should identify the use of simple and continuous forms in the examples.

3 Tell students that the best way to explain the meaning is to give a synonym.

Key

a *see* means 'understand' in the first sentence and 'have a relationship with' in the second.
b *think* means 'have an opinion' in the first sentence and 'intend/have a plan' in the second.
c *feel* means 'think/have an opinion' in the first sentence and 'experience an emotion' in the second.
d *have* means 'possess' in the first sentence and 'give birth to' in the second.

4 Key

1 've been sitting
2 are you doing/have you been doing
3 are always doing
4 enjoy
5 'll finish/'ll have finished

6 let

7 've never liked

8 'm thinking

9 'm having/'ve been having

10 means

11 doesn't fit

12 know

13 bites

14 've done

5 Suggested answers

a What **are** you **doing** this evening?

b How long **have** you **been learning** English?

c What do you usually **do** on Saturday evenings?

d Where do you think you'**ll be**/you'**ll be living** in ten years' time?

e What **were** you **doing**/**did** you **do**/**had** you **been doing** when the teacher came into the room?

Listening p50

1 Key

B

The phrases in bold in the Tapescript show where the answers can be located.

Tapescript 9

A Right, how many places have we been to in the hospital?

B Let's think. When we left the ward, I still had my bag. **So the first place was ... I know ... we waited beside the lifts for a while, didn't we?** The lift took ages to arrive.

A Then we went to the cafeteria. Did you have it then?

B Yes, I paid for the coffees. Then we went to the chemist's.

A And you still had it?

B Not sure. I've only just realised it's missing ...

A Hang on. *I* paid for the coffees! And I don't remember seeing your bag then.

B Really? **Let's go back to the first place**, then ...

2 The phrases in bold in the Tapescript show where the answers can be located.

Key

1 C

2 A

3 B

4 B

5 C

6 A

7 C

Tapescript 10

1

Emma Luke, I don't get this. Can you explain?

Luke Yes, look. Just move that equation over to this side, then the numbers come out equally.

Emma Oh, why don't I understand numbers?

Luke Well, everybody's different, Emma. I can't draw like you can, for example.

Emma But art's different. I just wish I were better at maths. It's not that I don't want to do it. I really concentrate when Miss Phipps is talking, but **after ten minutes I just don't follow any more. I'm not sure that Miss Phipps understands people who don't understand maths.**

Luke Well, after the exam you don't have to do maths any more.

Emma That doesn't help me now!

2

Gerard Sullivan isn't your average scientist, having a somewhat adventurous nature. Not for him the confines of a laboratory where he can study quietly with his microscope. Instead, he's a microbiologist who is fascinated by what can survive in extreme conditions. He's been in the Atacama desert, the driest place on earth, and in Antarctica, the coldest place, in search of the tiny microbes that survive in these inhospitable temperatures. They not only give us information about our amazing natural world, but also **vital clues about how life started on earth billions of years ago.**

3

A Sally! I'm stuck. I can't do this one. And I need it to **help me with this one across.** I'm nearly finished, but ...

B OK, what's the clue? Oh, that's tricky.

A Have you any idea? I don't know why I do these things. They're supposed to be good for the brain. They end up giving me a headache.

B You love them, really! Oh, wait a minute ... isn't it 'housework'?

A Well, that's what I thought, but then **five down doesn't fit anymore.**

B I see what you mean.

A Oh I need a break.

4

Ladies and Gentlemen, welcome. I hope that you have managed to pack some inspiration along with your brushes! If not, don't worry. We are here to inspire you! Ladies and gentlemen, think about how a child paints. Imagine a very young boy or girl with a piece of paper, a big brush and bright colours. **See how they take delight** in mixing new colours, applying the paint, experimenting with shape and design. **See how fearless they are.** They are totally absorbed in the *process* of painting, *not* the result. **It is the fun of the creative process that is the important thing. This is our aim for these classes.**

5

I wrote this song when I was seventeen. It's called 'Behind my back'. It's a bit embarrassing but I wrote it after my girlfriend secretly went out with my mate. When I found out, I was so hurt. I really loved her. And with my best friend! I couldn't understand why they would do that! **I couldn't forgive them. I confronted them and told them how I felt. They said that they didn't want to hurt my feelings, but that just made things worse. It was those feelings that prompted me to write the song.** Embarrassing, as I say, but I well remember how I felt then!

6

I love my job, though it's hard work and there's no money in it – unless you get a contract to supply the Queen! I have a small herd of sheep, and another of goats. My neighbour has a herd of cows, so **the raw materials aren't a problem**. Very little has changed over the centuries. We follow traditional recipes with the same ingredients. We only sell to independent shops. We don't supply any of the major supermarkets as they pay so little – **as little as 50p for a 100 gram packet of our leading brand. It costs us more than that to make it in the first place!**

7

A What are we going to get Dad?

B I don't know. He only likes taking the dog for a walk. Hey, walking boots?!

A A bit expensive. … . **Didn't he use to like reading about Antarctica?**

B Hasn't he got everything on the subject that was ever written?

A Oh, surely not. Or maybe there's a good DVD about it?

B Yes! A nature film! But which one?

A I wouldn't know how to choose … . Oh dear, what about those boots, after all?

B **Let's go with your original idea.** We can find something good, I'm sure. I'll look on the Internet, then **we can check his shelves**.

Speaking p51

1 Key

The tops of the skyscrapers are actually the pavement.

2 Key

a 2   b 1   c 2   d 1   e 1   f 1   g 1   h 2   i 1

3 Other useful words might include: *intricate*, *bold*, *ugly*, *in/out of proportion*, etc.

Suggested answer

They are both examples of urban art or 'street art', in other words they are outdoors. Both are colourful, large-scale works, and are 'free' in the sense that people do not have to pay to look at them. The first one looks more three-dimensional than the graffiti in the second one. It is unlikely that either artist has sought permission to draw or paint in a public space.

4 Key

a In the first photo, the artist has created the illusion of a three-dimensional scene below the pavement. We can see Spider-Man climbing up a building. The second photo is of graffiti sprayed onto a wall. The graffiti artists have sprayed large letters and other symbols which are difficult to read (called 'tags').

b Photo 1: to entertain and interest people; to take art onto the streets. Photo 2: to impress friends and other graffiti artists; to brighten up dull urban surroundings.

c Photo 1: drawn in chalk. It would be easy to remove with water. It will be washed away in any case the next time it rains.
Photo 2: spray paint (difficult to remove)

d The artist in photo 1 is very skilled, drawing in a fairly traditional style. The work of art is very original. The work of the graffiti artists is much more limited to letters and symbols, though these are often well formed.

5 Useful words for the discussion that you might want to elicit or pre-teach might include: *illegal, antisocial, self-expression, trend, prevention, vandalism, criminal damage,* etc.

Suggested answers

Vandalism: It costs a lot of money to remove it. It's unsightly. It causes damage to public buildings. The words that are sprayed are sometimes offensive.

Art: Many graffiti artists are highly skilled. It's a form of self-expression and can have a political dimension. It brightens up run-down urban areas.

Use of English p52

1 Key

a	6, 10, 10, 1	f	4, 6
b	11, 11	g	8, 8
c	1, 1, 4, 4	h	9
d	1	i	12, 8
e	5	j	10, 1, 4, 10

2 Key

a Leonardo da Vinci
b *The Last Supper,* the *Mona Lisa*
c a helicopter, a calculator, a tank

3 Key

1	a	7	later
2	the	8	the
3	about	9	one
4	As	10	of
5	was	11	did
6	whose	12	such

4 Key

a We use *a* to say what Leonardo da Vinci was.
b No article with some set phrases consisting of a preposition and noun.
c The use of *the* shows that there was only one Duke in Milan.
d No article with most countries.
e We use *the* when there is only one of something.
f We use *the* when there is only one of something, in this case a superlative.

Vocabulary p53

1 Check that students have remembered the significance of the 'separable' phrasal verb symbols ⟷ in the dictionary extract on page 47.

Key

a take sth back – Definition 1 (= 'return')
b take sb back (= 'allow to come home again')
c take sth back – Definition 2 (= 'to admit that what you said was wrong')
d take sb back (to …) (= 'to make somebody remember something')

2 Encourage students to attempt as many answers as possible before they check their dictionaries. Explain that when they do use their dictionaries, they should follow the advice in the **tip** box and scan the definitions for the right context.

Key

a	in	d	apart
b	off	e	up
c	on		

3 Key

(a–e below refer to the pairs of sentences in exercise 2)
a **take in** g and c
b **take off** h and b
c **take on** f and a
d **take apart** d and e
e **take up** j and i

Writing p54

1 When pairs have completed their discussion, ask them to report back to the class on their choices.

2 Students might disagree on which words are relevant, depending on which films they give as examples. Encourage discussion about this, if you have time.

3 Key

a Paragraph 3 c Paragraph 1
b Paragraph 4 d Paragraph 2

4 Explain that the present tense is sometimes used by reviewers to separate their description of what happens in the film from their reactions to it.

Key

The present simple

5 Key

a performances e stands
b set f short, miss
c impressed g tells
d fan, worth h spectacular

6 a e
b b, g
c a, c
d h
e d, f

Optional activity

Find other examples of authentic film reviews, either in newspapers and magazines or on the Internet, and get students to identify examples of the language covered in this section. (It might be best to do this **after** students have written their own reviews, in order to prevent them from directly copying the language.)

7 There is an an assessed authentic answer to this task on page 9 of the *Writing and Speaking Assessment Booklet*.

Review p56

1 Key

a light-hearted c powerful
b scary d gripping

2 Key

a shut down e think up
b hanging around f ended up
c started off g turn … into
d pick up

3 Key

1 the 10 –
2 the 11 –
3 – 12 –
4 the 13 –
5 – 14 a/the
6 a 15 the
7 the 16 a
8 a 17 the
9 a

4 Key

a in g on
b apart h off
c off i in
d back j up
e on k apart
f back

Real or fake?

Lead in p57

1 Students should be able to do this activity without needing to refer to a dictionary. Show them how grammatical clues can help them to find the right answers, e.g. the gap in number 1 has to be a verb in the infinitive and the one in 5 a past simple verb.

Key

1	pretend	6	tell
2	truthfully	7	forgery
3	honest	8	truth
4	own up	9	lie
5	cheated		

2 Encourage students to answer the questionnaire in complete sentences, rather than just giving yes/no answers. This should be in the form *We would/wouldn't … .*

3 Students should continue to work in pairs and write down some sentences in the form suggested in the question. Get students to read back some of their sentences.

Optional activity

This activity would lead naturally to a good class discussion, but this topic is revisited in the Writing section on page 66, so you might want to wait until then. Also, be aware that lying is a sensitive topic in some cultures.

Reading p58

1 Get students to attempt this task before consulting their dictionaries if necessary.

Key

a, b and h mean 'an action which is designed to deceive people'

b and d both mean 'a person who pretends to be somebody different in order to deceive people'

c and f both mean 'real and authentic'

e and g both mean 'to assume a false identity'

2 **Suggested answers**

Possible reasons include: for fun, to make money, to escape justice, to have a fresh start in life, to conceal one's background, to become famous, to deceive somebody into marriage, because of a psychological need, to open up career opportunities which would otherwise not exist.

3 Ask students to make a note of any reasons suggested in the text that they **hadn't** thought of while doing exercise 2. Then review both sets of reasons with the whole class.

Suggested answers

Arguably, 'James Barry' was an impostor for the sake of her career. Frédéric Bourdin seems to have been fulfilling a psychological need. Frank Abagnale probably did it for financial gain and also, perhaps, for entertainment. Archie Belaney probably did it to be famous, perhaps for fun and for financial gain too.

4 Get students to identify which part of each text they have based their answers on.

Key

1 C (l. 46)
2 B (l. 29–30; l. 36–37)
3 D (l. 76)
4 A (l. 6–7)
5 C (l. 60–61)
6 B (l. 26–27)
7 A (l. 4–6)
8 A (l. 12–13)
9 C (l. 58)
10 D (l. 72–73)
11 C (l. 64–66)
12 A (l. 3)
13 A (l. 2)
14 C (l. 62–63)
15 D (l. 88–90)

Vocabulary p60

1 Key

loud: bellow, scream, shriek, shout
quiet: grumble, mumble, murmur, mutter, whisper

2 Key

a shriek
b mutter
c grumble
d scream
e whisper

3

Students might have difficulty in identifying the correct prepositions. Remind them that, when they revise vocabulary, they need to learn the prepositions that are used with each verb.

Key

a about 3
b to   5
c on   1
d about 6
e to   4
f for   2

4

You could turn this into a game by getting students to read one of their completed sentences aloud. The rest of the class decide which of a–g it is.

Grammar p60

1 Key

a In 1, present simple changes to past simple. In 2, present continuous changes to past continuous. In 3, *will* changes to *would*. In 4, past simple changes to past perfect.
b These words all change in a logical way to reflect the change in point of view.
c *that*

2

Check that students understand the meaning of the reporting verbs in the list before they begin the activity.

Key

Speaker 1 He promised (that) he would do the washing-up the next day/the following day.

Speaker 2 She complained (that) she didn't like the TV programme/that TV programme.

Speaker 3 He boasted (that) he'd earned more than $1000 that day.

Speaker 4 She explained (that) she hadn't played tennis the day before because it had been raining.

Speaker 5 He predicted that something unexpected would happen (during) the coming week/the following week.

Speaker 6 She warned that the police were looking for him/her at that moment.

(Note: It's better not to omit 'that' in 5 and 6, to avoid initial grammatical ambiguity with 'he predicted something …', 'she warned the police …')

Tapescript 11

Speaker 1
Man I'll do the washing-up tomorrow morning.

Speaker 2
Woman I don't like this TV programme.

Speaker 3
Man I've earned more than $1,000 today!

Speaker 4
Woman I didn't play tennis yesterday because it was raining.

Speaker 5
Man Something unexpected will happen next week.

Speaker 6
Woman The police are looking for you at this moment!

3

If students are having difficulty, get them to try to answer d first. They should then be able to answer the preceding questions (a–c) by comparing the original questions with the reported questions.

Key

a no
b no
c if/whether
d 1 Where are my new shoes?
   2 What did you do yesterday?
   3 Do you want to come back tomorrow?

4 Suggested answer

Helen asked Mike what he was doing in her bedroom. Mike replied that he was looking for his mobile phone. He asked Helen if she'd borrowed it. She said that she'd never borrowed his mobile phone. Mike said/insisted that she'd used it the day before/the previous day. Helen said/insisted/claimed/explained that she hadn't made any calls. She explained that she had just been looking for a phone number. Mike asked her where she had left it. She replied/confessed that she couldn't remember. She asked Mike if he'd looked on the kitchen table. He insisted that he had looked everywhere.

Students will probably write a paragraph with lots of short sentences, many of them beginning 'Mike' or 'Helen'. Get them to make the paragraph flow more smoothly by using conjunctions to combine sentences, and pronouns to replace 'Helen' and 'Mike' once they have been mentioned at the beginning of the paragraph. For example:

Helen asked Mike what **her** was doing in her bedroom. **He** replied that he was looking for his mobile phone **and** asked **her** if she'd borrowed it. **She** said that she'd never borrowed his mobile phone **but he** said that she'd used it the day before/ the previous day. **She** said/insisted that she hadn't made any calls **and** explained that she had just been looking for a phone number. **He** asked **her** where she had left it. **She** replied that she couldn't remember **and** asked **him** if he'd looked on the kitchen table. **He** insisted that he had looked everywhere.

5 Key

a 'Please don't tell anyone.'
b 'Put your hands on your head!'
c 'Don't worry about anything.'
d 'OK, I'll help you with your homework.'
e 'I think you should apply for the job.'
f 'Do not contact the police.'

6 Remind students that they should use reported speech in their answers. If there's time, get pairs to report back to the class and check that they are using structures correctly in normal speech as well as in written exercises.

7 If students have dificulty in deciding on the correct verb forms, refer them to the Grammar Reference (p.166).

Key

1 to tell
2 he had played
3 was happening/had been happening
4 to explain
5 he had been impersonating
6 had started
7 I was
8 I wasn't

Listening p62

1 The clues lie in the fact that there needs to be a 'big contrast' between the person's real life and their fake one. Also, the example of the singer in a punk rock band becoming the conductor of a classical orchestra is actually reversed in this case.

2 Key

a The correct answer in 1 was a rock singer.
b no

Tapescript 12

Laura-Jane Foley, a twenty-year-old student at Cambridge University who sang in the university choir, took part in Series 5 of the TV programme, *Faking it*. Along with many other members of classical choirs around the country, Laura-Jane received an email about *Faking it*. She thought it sounded really exciting, so **she phoned the number in the email**. She did not really think that they'd be interested in her. But then, to her surprise, members of the TV company went to see her, and **soon after that, they were filming. From Laura-Jane's point of view, the whole thing happened amazingly quickly!**

Twenty-year-old Laura was a student at Cambridge University. She had never even been to a rock concert in her life, so it was going to need a huge transformation to make her into a convincing rock singer. The programme-makers decided that **her new identity would be called LJ** (the initials of her real name, Laura-Jane) – and that she would be the lead singer of a band called *Rehab*. In order to learn the skills and attitude necessary in just four weeks, Laura-Jane went to live with a girl called Harry, a real rock singer who enjoys living a rock-singer's lifestyle. But the two girls found it very difficult to get along – they were just too different. For Laura-Jane, this was the worst part of the whole experience. She explained that **she and Harry were both strong individuals, with strong opinions, and so big disagreements were inevitable.** For example, when Harry decided that Laura-Jane needed a new, shorter hairstyle, Laura-Jane refused. From Harry's point of view, Laura-Jane just wasn't trying. In fact, Harry couldn't understand why Laura-Jane had agreed to take part in the programme at all if she wasn't prepared to make changes – she suspected that Laura-Jane just wanted to be on television!

As part of her training, Harry took Laura-Jane to rock concerts. For example, on the second day of the four-week training period, they went to see American rock star Marilyn Manson. Laura-Jane confessed that she hadn't really enjoyed the experience at all. She complained that everyone had been dancing around, banging into each other. **She'd found the whole evening dangerous and scary.**

Nikki Lambourne, a singer who has performed with world-famous bands such as *The Who*, was employed to help Laura-Jane change and develop her style of singing. Laura-Jane got on with Nikki much better than with Harry, and she also liked the boys in her fake band, *Rehab*. She commented that they looked like punks, but were nice and really intelligent. It reminded her that your opinion of someone can't be based on what they look like. Unfortunately, because of the problems with her preparation, and in particular her bad relationship with Harry, Laura-Jane was not successful in fooling the judges at the end of the programme. After they had heard three different rock bands, two with genuine female rock singers and the other with Laura-Jane, **they correctly identified Laura-Jane as the 'fake'. So in that sense, her training was a failure.** And she admits that, although it was an amazing experience, she would not want to do it again. The rock world just didn't appeal to her, although she claims to have bought her first rock CD since the programme!

Laura says that the **whole experience of taking part in *Faking it* has made her more confident.** However, it has not changed her views on life – and it certainly has not made her more rebellious. She is still a respectable, classical-music-loving girl who sings in a choir – she's definitely not a rock chick!

3 Refer students to the **how to do it** box on page 14. Remind them that the words in the options will not be exactly the same as the ones they hear.

Key

1 A   2 C   3 C   4 B   5 A   6 C   7 B

The phrases in bold in the Tapescript show where the answers can be located.

4 Words you might want to elicit or pre-teach before this discussion include: *glamorous, creative, fame/famous, celebrity, to be good at/interested in, to have a talent for*, etc.

Speaking p63

1 Make sure students keep a note of the words they come up with, as you will need to refer back to them in exercise 2b.

2 **Key**

  a   Question c
  c   Possible answers include:
  Speaker 1: stay in contact, mobile phone
  Speaker 2: remember, three years old
  Speaker 3: clothes, personality
  Speaker 4: sea, tropical island, Zanzibar
  Speaker 5: broke down, couldn't fix, disaster

Tapescript 13

Speaker 1 [answering question b]
That's an interesting question. On balance, I think I am, because it's making life better. For example, it's much easier to stay in contact with your friends now that everybody has got a mobile phone.

Speaker 2 [answering question f]
Well, it's difficult to say, really, because I'm not sure whether I remember this, or whether people have told me about it. But if I think about it, I suppose one of the first things I remember is this: when I was about three years old, I ran away from home. Of course, I didn't get far – my dad followed me down the road, but I didn't see him.

Speaker 3 [answering question d]
It depends what you mean exactly. I guess the honest answer would be yes, because I always notice people's clothes, and I do think they say something about a person's character. But of course, other things – like personality – are more important.

Speaker 4 [answering question a]
That's tricky. I need to think for a moment. There are so many possibilities! I suppose the simplest answer to that question is 'by the sea'. Maybe a tropical island – like Zanzibar. I've always liked the sound of that.

Speaker 5 [answering question e]
Let me see. The best example that comes to mind is a recent trip to the mountains. Our car broke down on the way, and we had to call a garage. They couldn't fix the car, so in the end, we just went home again.

3 Once students have completed the matching task, point out the **tip** box and suggest that they memorise some or all of these expressions. You can also get them to practise saying some of the expressions aloud, focusing particularly on the ones that could sound rude if delivered with the wrong intonation (i.e. *I need to think for a moment, That's an interesting question, Let me see.*)

Key

I need to think for a moment.	4
That's an interesting question.	1
Well, it's difficult to say, really.	2
Let me see.	5
It depends what you mean, exactly.	3
I guess the honest answer would be …	3
I suppose the simplest answer to that question is …	4
If I think about it, I suppose …	2
On balance, I think …	1
The best example that comes to mind is …	5

Use of English p64

1 Most dictionaries will have a special way of marking these negative prefixes. In the *Oxford Advanced Learner's Dictionary*, the symbol **OPP** is used.

Key

a inactive   e impossible
b disallow   f insane
c illegal   g unsympathetically
d uninjured

2 Check that students understand the meaning of *sane* and *sympathetic* and their opposites. They should be able to infer from question a that *to be unsympathetic* means 'to be unkind to someone who is hurt', and from g that *insane* means 'mad'.

Key

a unsympathetically   e impossible
b uninjured   f inactive
c illegal   g insane
d disallow

3 **Key**

They are both computer-generated images.

4 **Key**

1 impossible   6 realistic
2 unaware   7 technological
3 actors   8 unlikely
4 impractical   9 disappear
5 immediately   10 unquestionable

Vocabulary p65

1 Get students to check their answers in their dictionaries.

Key

a 2   b 7   c 8   d 6   e 1   f 4   g 5   h 3

2 **Key**

a speaks out against
b talked down to us
c talk her out of
d get to the point
e got the wrong end of the stick
f talking about her behind her back
g talked me into
h speaks his mind

Writing p66

1 **Suggested answer**

A white lie is a lie which is told to protect somebody's feelings.

2 **Key**

a tell   d feel
b tell   e comes
c hurt

3 Explain that students don't need to use exactly the same ideas as their partner.

4 **Key**

paragraph 1 a   paragraph 3 d, e
paragraph 2 b, c   paragraph 4 f

5 Students' answers to this might vary, but g would normally be used in paragraph 1 and a, c or i in paragraph 4. (Phrases d and f are also 'introductory' phrases, but don't necessarily have to be used right at the beginning of the essay.)

Optional activity

Ask students to identify groups of phrases in the list (a–k) that have a similar function.
introducing a set of arguments: d, f and g;
introducing an idea or argument that follows on from the previous one: b, h and k;
introducing an idea or argument that contrasts with the previous one: e and j;
summarising and ending a set of arguments: a, c and i
You should point out that there is another group of phrases that is used to introduce existing facts and opinions, examples of which they can find in the language box.

6 **Key**

'It is true that …' is in the model answer.

7 Explain that the phrases in the language box fall into two categories. One type (*It is true that …*; *Nobody could deny that …*) is used to express facts and opinions that the writer believes are true, whilst avoiding using *I think* or *I believe* (see the **tip** box). The other type (e.g. *It is often said that …*; *It is sometimes suggested that …*) is often used to introduce a point of view which other people have, but which the writer wants to challenge.

8 There is an assessed authentic answer to this task on page 10 of the *Writing and Speaking Assessment Booklet*.

Review p68

1 Key

a boasted   d shouted
b confessed   e begged
c whispered   f insisted

2 Key

a He boasted that he earned five times as much as his brother.
b He confessed that he had lost the/those keys.
c She whispered in his ear that she had seen the film before.
d She shouted that her car was on fire.
e He begged him/her/them/me to stop singing.
f He insisted that he would be on time the next day/the following day.

3 Key

a uncivilised   e insincere
b inaccurate   f ungrateful
c illogical   g intolerant
d improbable   h disloyal

4 Key

a grateful   e illogical
b accurate   f sincere
c intolerant   g uncivilised
d loyal   h probable

5 Key

a out   d point
b out   e into
c end

6 Key

1 collector   6 following
2 examination   7 scientific
3 disappeared   8 carefully
4 connection   9 older
5 unbelievably   10 dishonest

Journeys

6

Lead in p69

1 This is a good opportunity to revise the prepositions used for different means of travel, e.g. *travel by plane/train/ship/bike*; *be on the train/a ship/a bike/foot/horseback*, etc.

2 Get the pairs to make notes during the different stages of discussion, and deal with any resulting vocabulary queries with the whole class.

3 This can be a pair or group discussion, or you could save it as an essay task for homework.

Reading p70

1 Limit this warm-up activity to five minutes.

2 Suggest to students that they follow the style of the example headlines on page 70.

Key

David Cornthwaite travelled across Australia on a skateboard. Possible headlines: 'Across Australia on a skateboard' or 'British man skateboards 5,800 km across Australia'.

3 Encourage students to explain the meanings of the phrases before checking in a dictionary.

Suggested answers

a 3 **epic journey:** a very long and challenging journey

b 1 **articulated lorry:** a long lorry which has two or more sections

c 5 **constant pain:** pain which does not stop

d 2 **four-wheel drive vehicle:** a vehicle in which the engine provides power to all four wheels

e 4 **motivational speech:** a speech which is intended to give people a more confident and positive attitude

Optional activity

Explain to students that these are examples of **collocations**: combinations of words that occur very often. Get them to check the different adjectives used in a–e in their dictionaries and see if the definitions given include the nouns they're used to describe. (e.g. in the *Oxford Advanced Learner's Dictionary*, they will find the phrase 'epic journey' in the definition of the adjective **epic**.)

4 Before doing the task, remind students about the **how to do it** box for *Multiple choice* on page 10.

Key

1 C He 'hated his job' (l. 7) and 'was looking for something new' (l. 9–10).

2 A It was successful because 'he finished … [in] just over a month' (l. 15–16), but painful because he had an infected blister.

3 D See l. 20–21.

4 A There were moments where he thought 'I have to rest' (l. 34–35) but he 'never contemplated giving up' (l. 35), which eliminates option B.

5 B His support team were in the four-wheel drive vehicle but he used 'camping equipment' (i.e. a tent) for night stops (l. 45).

6 C He 'hit a hole' (l. 50)

7 C See l. 56–57.

8 A A 'motivational speech'(l. 61) encourages people to feel more positive about themselves; it doesn't mean they have to copy what the speaker has done (this eliminates option D). Options B and C are also eliminated because another journey is 'on the cards' (= probable) and he's 'certainly not going back to the day job'.

5 Give the interviewers a little time to prepare questions but encourage the interviewees to make up their answers on the spot. Make sure they are using appropriate tenses for each of the three questions (a present, b past and c future), as well as for any other questions that the interviewers come up with.

Vocabulary p72

1 Key

a **platform**: the other three are all parts of an airport
b **overhead locker**: the other three are all bags that you take with you when you travel
c **wing**: the other three are parts of a boat
d **propeller**: the other three are people who work in transport
e **scooter**: the other three are vehicles that travel on water
f **ticket office**: the other three are travel documents

2 Key

a to board
b to pick up
c to get onto
d to change
e to cancel
f to get into

3

Check that students understand the expression *to cap it all* and perhaps teach the similar expression (*it was*) *the final straw*. Ask if they can think of an equivalent in their own language.

Key

1 ticket office
2 platform
3 ticket inspector
4 change
5 suitcases
6 check-in
7 departure lounge
8 board/get onto
9 overhead locker
10 hand luggage

Grammar p72

1 Key

a must
b should
c mustn't, can't
d ought to
e could, couldn't
f mustn't
g must

2

Encourage students to try to answer this without referring to the Grammar Reference explanation first.

Key

a should, ought to, must; the most emphatic is 'must'.
b must, mustn't
c could, can

3

Give students two or three minutes' preparation time. Remind them that when they're explaining their problems, they should turn the notes into complete sentences, and when they're giving advice, they should use a variety of the modal verbs they have just been practising.

4

You might need to give an example to accompany the **tip** box on page 73, e.g.

*My case was very heavy but I **managed to** carry it to the taxi.* (not … I could carry it … .) The activity in exercise 4 will then tell you whether students have understood the concept.

Key

I ~~could~~ *managed to* attract Harry's attention
I ~~could~~ *managed to* grab hold of the ladder

5 Key

a mustn't
b don't have to
c must
d have to
e don't have to
f mustn't

6 Suggested answers

1 can
2 don't have to
3 can
4 should/ought to
5 shouldn't
6 should/ought to
7 don't have to
8 can
9 must

Optional activity

In pairs, students brainstorm other ideas for green travel, which they can then present to the rest of the class.

Listening p74

1 Suggested answers

a boat/hovercraft/ferry
b car/taxi/bus/coach/bicycle/motorbike
c taxi/bus/coach
d car/taxi/bus/coach/motorbike
e bus/train/coach/tram
f bus/train/coach/tram/plane/ferry/hovercraft

2

Before looking at the text, remind students about the **how to do it** box for *Multiple choice* on page 50. The phrases in bold in the Tapescript show where the answers can be located.

Key

1 B
2 A
3 B
4 C
5 B
6 C
7 A

Tapescript 14

1

A This hotel is nearer the beach and has a shorter walk into town.

B **Perhaps it's better** to be nearer everything. **But won't it be noisier?**

A It won't be particularly noisy, as it's a small resort.

B I see. **It seems preferable** to the other one, **except perhaps it is better to be further outside the resort**, so you really feel far away from it all. But what's the beach like?

A Well, the beach nearest the hotel is shingle, but there are sandy ones further away.

B And does the other hotel have a sandy beach?

A Yes, it does.

B **Perhaps that one would be better after all …**

2

Mark Beaumont, adventurer and long-distance cyclist, is the subject of our programme today. **Mark was the first person ever to cycle the length of the Americas** from Alaska to the southern tip of Argentina. **He covered over 13,000 miles in 268 days and travelled through 20 countries, including one stretch of water.** On top of this, for good measure, **he climbed the highest peaks in North and South America** – Mount McKinley in Alaska at the beginning of his journey, and Aconcagua in Argentina, near the end. After nine months of riding through blizzards, forest fires and deserts, he was relieved to have finally made it.

3

It's six o'clock on Friday 25th November. Good evening. The Met Office has issued a severe weather warning for Scotland. South to south-westerly winds are expected to increase to severe gale force later this evening. Weather conditions will worsen overnight into tomorrow morning. **Non-essential car journeys should not be undertaken.** High winds will further disrupt travel during Saturday. **Ferry services and a freight flight have been cancelled.** If the conditions continue, schools will be closed on Monday, the council warned, as **buses for the pupils would not be allowed to run.**

4

The day I decided to row across the Atlantic, it was like a light went on in my head. I had been looking for a project for some time. I hate being bored, so I'm always setting myself challenges. When I'm on my deathbed, I want to be proud of what I've achieved. I want to do something memorable and, more than anything, I want to make a difference. If I rowed across an ocean by myself, other people would notice and **I could draw attention to the things I feel passionate about – pollution, renewable energy, and endangered species.**

5

This is the story behind my new transport idea – the electric unicycle. My grandad was an engineer. He had a workshop at the bottom of the garden and from a very young age I used to watch him. Later we started working together. **Before he died we were developing a new type of electric engine.** Then I visited China a couple of years ago. I was astonished by the pollution in the cities. I realised it was because of the millions of motorcycles there. So, when I got home, I immediately got to work to try and solve that problem, using the engine we'd built.

6

A Hello, customer services.

B I'd like to make a complaint.

A **Certainly. Name, please?**

B David Thomas. Well, I was travelling to work …

A **When was this?**

B Yesterday morning, but it wasn't the first time …

A **I understand. Time and destination?**

B Oh, 8.40 to Reading. As I said, I was travelling to …

A I'm sorry, I see that train was cancelled.

B Yes. I missed my …

A **Would you like a refund?**

B What? Yes, but this isn't the first time …

A Well, sir, I'm happy to send you a complaints procedure form with your refund, **if you can just give me your address …**

B Oh … OK … Thank you.

7

A Hi Sally. What happened to you?

B I fell off my bike. Well, I got my bike out. But the chain fell off! So I borrowed my brother's.

A Are you ok?

B I've got a bruise on my knee, but otherwise I'm OK.

A What about the bike?

B I've bent the front wheel. **Simon will be so upset. He's racing on Saturday. I don't think it'll be fixed in time.**

A Oh, dear. I think you should get a doctor to look at your knee.

B No, it's only bruised. It's almost stopped hurting.

3 Encourage the students asking the questions to make up more questions of their own and to ask supplementary questions arising from their partner's replies. Also, ask the students being interviewed to reply in complete sentences.

Speaking p75

1 This can be done either as a whole class or in pairs. Check that students are using different forms of 'speculating' language in their discussion, e.g. *It's probably ...* , *It may/could/might be ...* , etc.

Key

a the helicopter trip
b the desert safari
c the tombs of the pharaohs
d the day trip to Alexandria

2 Suggested answers

1 helicopter ride (exciting, uncomfortable, windy, view, heights)
2 Alexandria (city, coach, swim, sea)
3 desert safari (48 hours, sand, scenery)
4 the tombs of the pharaohs (ancient ruins, fun, bad-tempered animals)
5 Nile adventure (relaxing, riverboat)

Tapescript 15

1

Man This looks like an exciting excursion, don't you agree?
Woman Not really. I'm not sure I like the look of it!
Man Oh? Why not?
Woman It could be a really uncomfortable ride. It's very windy.
Man I suppose so. But just think of the view!
Woman I'm sorry, I'm sure I'd feel sick. And I don't really like heights, either.

2

Man This one seems like the best option to me.
Woman Really? Why?
Man Well, it's a city I've always wanted to visit. I've read about it in books.
Woman It's quite a long way away, though. We'd be on a coach for a couple of hours each way.
Man I'm sure it will be worth it. And we might even get to swim in the sea!
Woman Well, OK. You've persuaded me! Let's book it.

3

Woman Have you decided yet?
Man No, I haven't. I'm still looking.
Woman If you ask me, I really think we should try this one.
Man You don't think it could get boring – 48 hours looking at sand?
Woman Not at all. Believe me, the scenery will be spectacular.
Man Well, OK then. Let's find out how much it costs.
Woman Great! I'll ask at reception.

4

Man I'm really keen on the idea of seeing some ancient ruins.
Woman Sure, but there must be a better way to get there!
Man Oh, come on! That's part of the fun!
Woman Really? I've heard they're very bad-tempered animals.
Man I'm sure these particular ones aren't.
Woman Well, OK, I suppose we could try it. But only if I get to choose the next excursion.
Man It's a deal.

5

Woman Shall we book an excursion for tomorrow?
Man Yes, OK. What kind of thing?
Woman Personally, I'm in favour of something relaxing! I'm really tired after all the sightseeing today.
Man Well, how about this one? What could be more relaxing than spending a few hours on a riverboat?
Woman Hmm. Maybe. I wonder what the food will be like, though.
Man I expect there'll be a buffet. It'll be fine. Let's go for it.
Woman Oh, OK.

3 Key

a 2 b 3 c 5 d 3 e 2 f 5 g 1 h 4 i 1 j 4

4 Explain to students that these expressions are typically used in 'decision-making' discussions, and that they can help improve their performance in Speaking Part 3.

5 If you can find English-language brochures or websites for tourism in your country, you could use this as source material for this activity.

Use of English p76

1 Get students to match as many as they can, then allow them to use a dictionary to help them complete the exercise. Students may have difficulty in distinguishing between *while/whereas* and *seeing that/since*. Explain that the former expresses contrast ('but') and the latter consequence ('because'), giving other examples if necessary.

Key

a 3 b 6 c 1 d 5 e 4 f 2

2 Key

a Passengers must sit (*or* remain seated) while the coach is moving.
b Phone me if you know that your flight will be late.

c   Travelling by taxi is more expensive (*or* dearer) than travelling by bus./Travelling by bus is not as expensive as travelling by taxi.

d   The cheaper seats are more uncomfortable.

e   When there is not much traffic, the journey is faster/quicker.

f   The use of mobile phones is not allowed (*or* permitted) during the flight.

3 Key

Remind students that contracted forms, e.g. *isn't* count as two words, i.e. *is not*.

a   We should get to the hotel by 9pm <u>provided the flight isn't</u> late.

b   Take some money with you <u>in case you need</u> to get a taxi.

c   Last year's holiday <u>was more fun than</u> this year's.

d   Travellers can <u>only bring pets</u> into the UK if they have a 'pet visa'.

e   The journey <u>wasn't as bad</u> as I'd expected.

f   That ferry looks <u>as though it's leaning</u> to one side.

Vocabulary p77

1   Explain that the phrases may be in a dictionary under *come* and *go* or another part of the phrase (e.g. *scratch* for *come up to scratch*.)

Key

a	come	e	come
b	come	f	goes
c	go	g	went
d	comes	h	came

2   *When it comes to ...* and *As far as ... go(es) ...* have a similar meaning, but students should work out the answers from the word order.

Key

1   When it comes to holidays
2   As far as cruise ships go
3   Things went from bad to worse
4   What came to mind
5   Complaining doesn't come easily to me
6   didn't come up to scratch
7   just goes to show
8   a dream come true

Writing p78

1 Key

(1) Is there a lot to do in August. (2) What's the best way to get to your house? (3) Do (your parents) like chocolates?

2 Key

Maria has followed all the advice except: 'Don't include any unnecessary information.' (Her first paragraph contains unnecessary information about mutual friends.)

3 Key

a   dying to
b   check out
c   stuff like that
d   loads of

4 Key

Whatever you do, don't ..., Make sure you ..., you'd be best off ...

5   There is an assessed authentic answer to this task on page 11 of the *Writing and Speaking Assessment Booklet*.

Review p80

1 Key

a   visa
b   ferry, scooter
c   bus driver, ticket
d   flight attendant, hand luggage, overhead lockers

2 Key

a	pick up	d	cancelled
b	change	e	board
c	got into		

3 Key

a   You must wear a helmet when you're riding a motorbike.

b   From our first floor apartment, we could hear noises in the street below.

c   We couldn't reach the airport in time.

d   May I have a seat by the aisle?

e   You shouldn't drink the tap water when you're staying in a hotel.

f   You don't have to tell me, I already know where you've been!

g   Only seven students managed to finish the exam within the time allowed.

h   She should (*or* ought *or* must) visit the Eye museum while she's in Brazil.

4 Key

1   as well as
2   whereas
3   since

4   as though
5   in order that
6   whether

5 Key

a   The hotel room really <u>didn't come up to</u> scratch.

b   It was a bumpy flight, and things <u>went from bad</u> to worse after we'd landed.

c   When my parents asked what I wanted for my birthday, <u>nothing came to</u> mind.

d   My sister is not bad at tennis, although ball games <u>don't come easily</u> to her.

I get the message

Lead in p81

1 Ask each pair to report back and see which forms of communication seem to be the most and least popular.

2 **Suggested answers:**

a

Email, text messages, instant messaging and chatrooms are probably more popular with younger people. The others are arguably more popular with older people.

Younger people have grown up with computers and mobile phones and are often unafraid of, or even keen to embrace, new technology. They are also perhaps more impatient than older people and like the quick response you can get with instant messaging, email, etc. Chatrooms are also a way of making new friends, which appeals to young people.

Older people are perhaps more resistant to change and stick with methods of communication that they know well, such as letters, phone and postcards. Some have difficulty getting to grips with new technology.

b

Email: Advantages: Fairly quick. No need to leave the house. Can email from a laptop while on the move. Good for business correspondence. Costs nothing once you have an Internet connection. Disadvantages: May receive junk mail. Technology not always reliable. Less personal than a note, letter or phone call.

Letter: Advantages: Personal. Nice to keep. Good for business where you need a record of the communication. Good for formal correspondence. Disadvantages: Usually takes longer to write. Have to post it. Have to buy paper and stamps.

Postcard: Advantages: Quick and easy way to stay in touch. Nice to see a photo of where somebody is on holiday. Disadvantages: Sometimes arrives after the sender has returned home. Anyone can read it.

Text message: Advantages: Can be very quick. Easy to write, especially with predictive text. Good for quick, informal communication. Cheap. Disadvantages: Limited length. Possibly open to misinterpretation if message is too brief. Depends on person having their phone switched on.

Phone: Advantages: Immediate response (if the person is there). Personal. Can avoid misunderstandings as information can be checked at the time – therefore probably very quick to successfully achieve purpose of call. Usually quite cheap but depends on service, time of day, etc. Can be formal or informal. Disadvantages: May take more time than e.g. an email as may have to discuss irrelevant information. Not always convenient for the personal you are calling to talk. No record of the details you have discussed if it's a formal business call.

Blogging: Advantages: Easy and inexpensive to create, maintain and update. Can look very professional. A fun way of sharing your ideas widely. With an Internet connection can be updated wherever you are. Disadvantages: You may post something which you later regret, and which is quite difficult to delete.

Social networking: Advantages: Good way of keeping in touch with friends and family. You can meet new people with similar interests. Easy to exchange files and photos and information about common interests. Free to use. Disadvantages: Can be time-consuming (and is banned in many workplaces). Not always secure – personal details can be used in identity theft. Replaces personal contact.

Chatroom: Advantages: Easy and informal way to meet people with similar interests. Free to use. Disadvantages: Need to be careful who you chat with. You can't be sure people are who they say they are.

Reading p82

1 Students can do this on their own or in pairs. Make sure they know the names of the objects and get them to report back to the whole class using sentences beginning with *You could* ….

2 Ask students if they were surprised by any of the other techniques mentioned in the text and, if so, why.

The matches can be used to light a fire (A).
The mirror can be used to reflect the sun (B).

The branches can form patterns (C).
The blanket / piece of cloth can be made into patterns (C).

Suggested answer

If the pilot hasn't seen the message, he obviously isn't going to signal that he hasn't seen it.

3 Key

1 B (l. 24–25)
2 A (l. 7)
3 A (l. 16–17)
4 D (l. 40)
5 D By definition, body movements don't require equipment or materials.
6 A (l. 11–12)
7 C (36–37)
8 B (l. 19–20)
9 C (l. 32–33)
10 A (l. 10–11)
11 D (l. 45–46)
12 C (l. 38–39)
13 B (l. 27–28)
14 B (l. 22)
15 D (l. 46)

4 Suggested answers

A rainforest: Start a fire. Find a clearing and make letters by digging or with branches.
A desert: Make big letters in the sand.
A mountain range: Start a fire. Make letters in the snow.
A grassy plain: Start a fire. Make letters in the grass, by digging or perhaps by flattening the grass.

Vocabulary p84

1

You could do this activity as a game of 'Snap'. Get students to work in pairs and give them five minutes to write down as many answers as possible. One pair then shouts out their answers, with other groups shouting out 'Snap!' if they have the same answer. The pair with the most answers not found by any other group wins.

2 Key

a 2   b 5   c 4   d 1   e 3   f 6   g 7

Optional activity

Get students to write similar sentences with the other uses of *get* from exercise 1. Collect the sentences, check them, then compile a test using the students' own sentences. You can give them this test for homework/revision, perhaps before they do the **Use of English** section on page 88, which also deals with uses of *get*.

Grammar p84

1

If students don't understand the task, do the first question with the whole class.

Key

1 are carrying out
2 believed
3 think
4 export
5 can block
6 replace
7 will set up

2

Students may be able to identify the correct verbs but have difficulty putting them into the correct form, in which case refer them to the relevant sections of the Grammar Reference.

Key

1 was arrested
2 was caught
3 were discovered
4 is being held
5 has been fined
6 being convicted
7 was stopped
8 was found

Optional activity

Check that students understand **why** the passive is used in these two paragraphs. The actions are carried out by the police, who would normally therefore be the subject of each sentence. But, in each paragraph, the main focus of interest is the criminal, which is why the passive verbs are preferred. Refer students to the Grammar Reference on Use of the Passive (note 2, p.170).

3 Key

Examples: Stolen phones can be blocked, SIM cards can easily be replaced

a can/could be seen

b mustn't be worn

c should be completed

d should never have been allowed

e might not have been killed

f must have been posted

4 Explain to students that we use these structures when we're focusing on what is believed, but not on who believes it.

Key

a it was believed that

b Over 200 mobile phones an hour are thought to have been stolen

5 Key

a It was reported that a coach collided with a lorry on the motorway last night.

   A coach was reported to have collided with a lorry on the motorway last night.

b It was thought the politician was telling the truth.

   The politician was thought to have been telling the truth.

c It is believed the police have arrested the wrong man.

   The police are believed to have arrested the wrong man.

   The wrong man is believed to have been arrested by the police.

d Mary is expected to pass all her exams.

   It is expected that Mary will pass all her exams.

e He is considered to be one of the finest writers alive.

   It is considered that he is one of the finest writers alive.

f It is believed that the woman was driving too fast when she crashed into the tree.

   The woman is believed to have been driving too fast when she crashed into the tree.

6 Point out that the indirect object is usually a person (see Grammar Reference on 'Verbs with two objects', p.170.)

Key

a Two: *me* is the indirect object, *£50* is the direct object.

b The indirect object.

7 Point out that the agent, preceded by *by*, normally comes at the end. (see Grammar Reference on 'Verbs with two objects', page 170.)

Key

a We are taught English by Mr Fielding.

b I'll be sent a receipt in the post by the online store.

c He has been given two days by the kidnappers to pay the ransom. (or ... to pay the ransom by the kidnappers).

d The children were read a bedtime story by my wife.

e She was brought two letters to sign by her secretary.

Listening p86

1 The phrases in bold in the tapescript show where the answers can be located.

Key

1 D   2 A   3 E   4 C   5 F

The extra item is B.

Tapescript 16

Speaker 1

There was a big sales conference coming up and our boss called us all to a meeting about it. I was tired, having been out late with my friends the night before, and I don't think I was really listening properly. Anyway, we were all given our products to present and we had to prepare a talk and demonstration to present to the sales force. I decided to work really hard on my own to create a good impression on my boss. On the day of the meeting, one of my colleagues got up first and presented *my* product. I was shocked! I tried to find my boss to find out what was happening. **It turned out that I had prepared the wrong talk for the wrong product.** I was horrified, and it was my turn next to speak. I had to make an apology in front of my boss. It was terrible. I've always paid attention in meetings since then.

Speaker 2

Last week I went to the cinema with my friend Becky. I should say at this point that I'm new to the city, having only moved here a couple of months ago. Anyway, we'd arranged to meet at ten to seven outside the Odeon cinema. I was a bit late but there was still plenty of time before the film started, so that wasn't a problem. What was a problem was that Becky didn't turn up. I waited till seven and then rang her on her mobile. 'Where are you?' she says. I tell her I'm outside the Odeon cinema and ask her where she is. She says she's outside the Odeon too. 'You can't be,' I say. **What I didn't know was that there are two Odeons in Oxford and I'd got the wrong one.** Luckily they aren't far apart and so Becky gave me directions to the other cinema. We had a good laugh about it later.

Speaker 3

We hadn't got any plans for New Year's Eve and my girlfriend and I were wondering what to do. We'd rung a few friends to see if they were at a loose end but everyone seemed to have plans. Finally I asked a couple we'd met fairly recently – Rob and Rosie – if they were doing anything. I spoke to Rob on the phone and he said they usually got together with a set of old friends from university but why didn't we pop round for a drink and a bite to eat with them in the evening. So we turned up about eight thirty and walked in on a dinner party in full swing! And it was obvious we weren't expected as there weren't any spare places at the table. Anyway, **apparently Rob had said New Year's Day on the phone, so we were 24 hours early.** They were really nice about it and made us feel welcome, but I felt terrible and just wanted the floor to swallow me up. It was so embarrassing.

Speaker 4

It was about three months ago, I guess, and we'd been invited to my brother's for the weekend. He'd just moved house so we hadn't been there before. He rang me beforehand and told me how to get to his cottage which is in a small village in the middle of nowhere. So we set off and I didn't bother to check where we were going on the map. We got hopelessly lost because **I'd written down the wrong road – I thought my brother had said follow the A214, but he swears he said the A241.** Anyway, we got there in the end, but about two hours late!

Speaker 5

I'd just got this new job in a big advertising agency. I think I'd been there about a week. I got an email from my boss about a departmental meeting. The email wasn't addressed directly to me but seemed to be copied to the people in my department. So naturally I assumed I should attend. I set off for the meeting, but I didn't know exactly where the room was and I got a bit lost on the way, so I arrived about five minutes late. I walked into the meeting room, and everybody stopped talking and stared at me. I just said, 'Sorry, I'm late.' **And my boss thanked me quite kindly, but said that I needn't be there.** I felt awful and turned completely red from embarrassment. It turned out that they needed to discuss what projects they were going to give me! I felt such a fool.

2 Key

a	set	d	turned
b	written	e	got, pop
c	turn	f	coming

Speaking p86

1 Possible answers

Advantages: You can speak English outside the classroom. You can meet and speak with lots of native speakers. You can learn about the culture of the country you are visiting. You can probably meet students from different countries.

Disadvantages: It may be expensive. It may be difficult to find out if the school is any good. You may get homesick. You may not get on with the host family. You may not like the food.

2 Suggested answers

a   Advertisement 1 would appeal to people who enjoy outdoor activities, but would have little appeal for less sporty people. Advertisement 2 would appeal to teenagers who like going out at night. However, it would be less successful with quieter people who prefer the company of just one or two good friends. Advertisement 3 is likely to appeal to all teenagers. Advertisement 4 will appeal to students who are serious about language learning, but will be less attractive to those who see the time they will spend at the school as a holiday. Advertisement 5 would appeal to people who are interested in learning about the lifestyle and culture of the country they are visiting and who really want to make an effort to speak English outside the classroom. Those students who prefer to spend most of their time with people of their own age and/or nationality would be less impressed.

b   Advertisements 3 and 2 would probably attract the most students, but students can give any opinions.

3 Key

The examiner asks questions a and d.

The female student gives better answers as she comes up with her own ideas, whereas the male student tends to reproduce phrases from the advertisements.

Tapescript 17

Examiner Would you like to take a course at this language school?
Female student Yes, I would.
Examiner Why?
Female student Well, I'd like to improve my English. I think that the best way to do that is to spend time in an English-speaking country.
Examiner And what about you?
Male student I agree.
Examiner You'd like to take a course at this school?
Male student Yes, I would. Because I would really enjoy it.
Examiner Why do you think it's important to study foreign languages?
Male student Because you can meet people from different countries and you can learn about their cultures and customs.
Examiner I see. Do you agree?
Female student Yes, I do. I also think it's particularly important to learn English.
Examiner Why?

Female student Because English is an international language. For example, if I meet someone from Poland, I can't speak Polish, and they probably can't speak Italian. But we can communicate in English.

4 Encourage students to listen to each other carefully and take notes during the conversation.

Suggested answers for questions c and d in exercise 3.

c   Non-native speakers may have a better understanding of the problems their students will face. They are able to explain difficult concepts in the native language. They may be better at putting students at their ease in the classroom.
Native-speaker teachers can have a better command of English than non-native speakers (but non-native speaker teachers sometimes have a better knowledge of formal grammar because they've studied English as a foreign language). And native-speaker teachers can sometimes provide better models, especially in pronunciation and intonation.

d   English is used across the world in commerce, science, aviation, education, diplomacy, etc. A knowledge of English makes it relatively easy to do business with people of almost any other nationality. Being able to speak English opens up more job opportunities. If you can understand English you can read English literature and watch English-language films in their original form. It also enables you to make friends with people from English-speaking countries and with people from other countries whose first language you do not speak.

Use of English p88

1 Key

a   How did you *get out of* going to that dreadful party?

b   What page have you *got up to* in the book you're reading?

c   We've *got through* six litres of milk since your parents arrived.

d   Give me a break, will you? You're always *getting at* me.

e   What really *gets* me *down* about winter is the long cold evenings.

f   What time does your flight *get in*?

g   'Grandad's getting very forgetting forgetful.'
    'Well, he's *getting on*, isn't he?'

3 Key

1 D
2 D   (*rather than* would be correct)
3 C
4 B
5 B
6 C
7 A   *sum*, rather than *amount*, is used for a precise amount of money mentioned in a bill.
8 C   (*got into the national news* would be correct)
9 A
10 C
11 A
12 D

Vocabulary p89

1 Key

a   *omit*. Formal – reads like an exam rubric.

b   *lock him up*. Informal – strong personal opinion, spoken.

c   *Speed up*. Informal speech, child to parent.

d   *returning, requesting*. Formal written letter of complaint.

e   *work out*. Informal spoken.

f   *vacate*. Polite formal written notice.

2 Students may use formal verbs when the phrasal verb equivalent would have been more appropriate. Suggest they learn new phrasal verbs with their formal equivalent, and vice versa.

Key

1   I'd love to *find out* why Jack *turned down* the offer of a free holiday with me, so try to *bring up* the topic when you speak to him!

2   We *set off* early in the morning, but we *ran into* heavy traffic on the motorway, which really *held* us *up*.

3   *Hang on* a minute. Are you saying that you *sent in* the application form without *filling in* your name and address?

4   My brother didn't *own up* to breaking the window – instead he *made up* some story about two men throwing a brick then *making off* on a motorbike.

Writing p90

1 Elicit or teach students *lose touch with, get together with, meet up with,* before they begin the discussion. Explain that *get together with* and *meet up with* sound less formal than *meet.*

2 Key

2, 4, 1, 3

3 Key

a came back, get down to, meet up

b that's, can't, didn't, you're, don't

c a couple of, a bit of, can't wait to, mates, great

d The whole of paragraph 3, for example.

e Can't wait to see you again! Yes, I do remember you! It would be really great to see you again!

f Can't wait to see you again!

4 Suggested answer

Got your email a couple of days ago. I'm glad that you're having a good time but was sorry to hear that they turned down your application to go to university. What a shame! When will you find out if you can study at another university instead? Anyway, please, please write back soon! Hope to see you again before too long.

5 Key

Reacting to the input: b, d
Finishing an email: a, f
Signing off: c, e

6 Tell students that, while they can use some of the expressions in the model emails on page 90, they shouldn't copy from them directly. Also, remind them that they need to use some of the informal language features covered in exercise 3.

There is an assessed authentic answer to this task on **page 12 of the** *Writing and Speaking Assessment Booklet.*

Review p92

1 Key

a I couldn't make the shop give me a refund.

b Tom's very lucky – he never suffers from coughs or colds.

c I really don't understand what you're saying.

d The ship became/grew smaller and smaller before disappearing over the horizon.

e What time did you arrive home last night?

f Sam achieved the highest possible score in his music exam.

g When did you buy that digital camera?

2 Key

a out of	e through
b down	f at
c on	g in
d up to	

3 Key

a 5 b 6 c 4 d 1 e 2 f 3

4 Key

a work out

b made up

c accelerate

d set off

e turned down

f Own up

5 Key

1	much	5	up
2	do	6	would
3	used	7	can't
4	since	8	up

A matter of taste

Lead in p93

1 You could ask students which words helped them identify the right answers and write them on the board under different headings: ingredients, utensils, ways of cooking.

Key

1   E   Italy
2   B   Japan
3   C   Hungary
4   D   India
5   A   Spain

Tapescript 18

1
You make some dough with flour and water and roll it flat. Then you make a tomato sauce with onion, garlic and herbs and spread the sauce on the dough. Sprinkle on some cheese and other things like olives and ham – anything you like really. Then bake it in the oven.

2
You boil the rice and add some vinegar and a little sugar and salt. Then, while the rice is cooling, slice the fish very thinly. Now, pick up a small amount of rice in your hand – it's best to wet your hands so that it doesn't stick to them – and mould the rice into an oval shape. Then lay a piece of fish along it.

3
It's very easy to make. You need some beef or lamb, onions, green peppers, tomatoes, paprika – those are basic ingredients anyway. It's best to fry the onions and beef for a few minutes first, then put everything into a large casserole with some water. Put it in the oven for a couple of hours and it's ready.

4
There are lots of different versions of this dish, but this is a quick and easy one. First chop up the onions, garlic, green pepper, and fry them in oil. Then stir in the chillis and ginger, and the spices – cumin, coriander and turmeric. Then add the pieces of chicken and stir them round so they're covered in the sauce. Cook it for about 20 or 30 minutes. Finally add a couple of spoonfuls of yoghurt. Then serve it with rice.

5
There are loads of ingredients, but the basic ones are rice, seafood, chicken, spicy sausage, pepper and onion. It's quite complicated, but I'll tell you roughly what to do. First you fry the onions, sausage and pepper in a large flat pan, and grill some chicken legs. Then add the rice and chicken to the pan, with some stock. Cook it for about 15 minutes and add the seafood towards the end.

2 Elicit or preteach some additional vocabulary for recommending food, e.g. *tasty*, *delicious*, *filling*, *moreish*.

3 Elicit or pre-teach some of the vocabulary of food description needed for the different categories in b, (see the suggested answers for **Vocabulary** exercise 1 on page 96, where this is covered in more detail).

Reading p94

2 Key

At 'Dans le Noir' diners eat in the dark and are served by blind waiters and waitresses.
At 'The Fat Duck', diners can eat a seafood dish while listening to the sound of the sea through an iPod.
The photo shows people going into 'Dans le Noir' in the dark and holding on to each other as they cannot see where they are going.

3 Key

1   C   Students should look for a sentence beginning *They ...* to follow on from *two restaurant owners* (1.3). The use of *they* in the following sentence confirms this grammatical link.

2   A   Students should look for a sentence beginning *He ...* to follow on from *Edouard de Broglie, the restaurateur* (1.8); the topic match means they should eliminate B.

3   H   Students should look for a sentence beginning *Some ...* to complete the contrast with *Others* (1. 12).

4   G   This makes a topic match with the surrounding sentences.

5   B   Students should look for a sentence beginning *He ...* to follow on from *Heston Blumenthal* (1. 31) and the link between *adventurous* and *experimental* and the food mentioned in B.

6   F   Students should get this mainly through the topic match with the surrounding sentences.

7 D Students should look for a sentence beginning *The first ...*, which is then followed by *The second* (1. 58).
Extra sentence: E

Vocabulary p96

1 Suggested answers

Positive: *tasty, tender,*
Neutral: *bitter, chewy, crunchy, fatty, mild, plain, rich, salty, spicy, sweet*
Negative: *greasy, stodgy, tasteless.* The following adjectives could be negative if the food is not supposed to have these qualities: *bitter, chewy, fatty, greasy, plain, salty, sweet.*

2 Suggested answers

curry: mild, rich, spicy, tasty
olives: bitter, salty, tasty
ice-cream: rich, sweet, tasty
fried chicken: chewy, fatty, greasy, tasty, tender
steak: chewy, fatty, tasty, tender
boiled rice: plain, stodgy, tasteless
coffee: rich, bitter, sweet, mild, tasty

3 Key

fried	3
boiled	7
roast	6
grilled	2
barbecued	1
baked	5
stewed	4

Optional activity

Find examples of authentic restaurant menus in English that give descriptions of how food is cooked. Look at the language and get students to write menus of their own, perhaps including local dishes.

Grammar p96

1 Get students to say the sentences (1–6) out loud. Teach them that when *can't* is used with the meaning *I'm sure it isn't true*, it is always stressed in speech.

Key

1 That fish <u>can't</u> be cooked yet. It's only been under the grill for two minutes.
   I'm sure it isn't true that ...; present
2 This meat is a bit dry and chewy. The chef <u>must have</u> overcooked it.
   I'm sure it's true that ...; past
3 There were three tins of olives in the cupboard. We <u>can't have</u> eaten them all, can we?
   I'm sure it isn't true that ...; past
4 Don't take the chicken out of the freezer yet. We <u>might</u> be eating out tonight if I can book a table.
   It's possibly true that ...; present
5 You haven't eaten a thing since yesterday lunchtime. You <u>must</u> be starving.
   I'm sure it's true that ...; present
6 I feel really ill. I think I <u>might have</u> eaten something that disagreed with me.
   It's possibly true that ...; past

2 Key

a He might give you a ring this evening.
b Patricia can't be wearing her scarf. I saw it hanging on the hook on the back door.
c James must have my mobile. I let him use it to call his sister this morning.
d That can't be Jim over there. His hair isn't as long as that.
e I might be able to give you a hand with the cooking if I get home in good time.

3 Suggested answers

a You might be going down with something./You might have caught a virus.
b You must be joking./You can't have done!/You must be terrified.
c You must be looking forward to it./You must have lots of money!
d He must be feeling terrible./He can't have been doing his job very well.
e You must be feeling upset./You can't be feeling very happy.
f You must be feeling fed up./You can't be serious.

4 Key

a must have eaten
b can't have stirred
c might have been invented
d must have spent
e must/might have left
f can't have written down
g must have spilt

5

Get students to do this on their own or in pairs and then review answers with the whole class.

Suggested answers

1 He must be hungry. He might be taking part in an eating competition. He must like hot hot dogs. He might get fat. He can't possibly enjoy eating all those hot dogs. Someone must have spent a lot of time making all those hotdogs.

2 It must be someone's birthday. The party must be over. It might have been a party for a one-year-old baby. It must have been a delicious cake.

3 They might be celebrating something. It might be someone's birthday. It might be an office party. The restaurant staff must be very busy. They must be having a good time.

Listening p98

1

Allow about five minutes for this warm-up activity. Make sure students take turns in asking and answering questions.

2

The phrases in bold in the Tapescript show where the answers can be located.

Key

1 C 2 B 3 F 4 A 5 E
Extra letter: D

Tapescript 19

Speaker 1
What a disaster last Thursday was! It was Valentine's Day and I wanted to treat my girlfriend, so I booked a really posh restaurant in the city centre. I went to pick her up in the evening in a taxi, and she came out of the house looking beautiful in a new dress. We got to the restaurant, which looked lovely with candles and roses everywhere, and went in. But the restaurant had absolutely no record of our booking! They were so apologetic, but they were completely full, as was every other nice restaurant in town that

evening. **We ended up going home to my place and eating a pizza from the freezer.** We laughed about it but it was so disappointing, really.

Speaker 2
We both got home from work last Friday feeling a bit tired. Neither of us could face doing the cooking so on the spur of the moment we decided to eat out. We caught the bus into town wondering if we would get a table anywhere, as it's always quite busy on Fridays. But we decided that we'd get a takeaway if we were unlucky. When we got to our favourite Thai restaurant, it was really busy. But the waiter kindly said that **if we came back in an hour, he'd squeeze us in! So we had a drink in the pub across the road, then had a great meal,** and went home feeling all happy and relaxed.

Speaker 3
My parents wanted to take me out for dinner last week to celebrate passing my exams, but they booked a restaurant on the evening of our class party, which wasn't a good idea! I was having such good fun at the party that I stayed till the end and didn't get home till 7.30, which was when the table had been booked for! So we rushed into town and got there at ten past eight. Fortunately for me, the restaurant had kept our table. The only problem was **that the service was really slow.** But we couldn't really complain because we'd been late in the first place!

Speaker 4
I went out with my friends at the weekend for a meal. We wanted to eat Chinese for a change, so my friend Tom had booked the restaurant for all eight of us. We all went to the 'Jasmine Flower Garden' as Tom had told us to, but when we got there, the restaurant couldn't find any record of our booking! Tom was a bit cross, and insisted that he had booked the table, but it turned out that **he had actually booked their sister restaurant the 'Jasmine Flower Palace' on the other side of town!** Tom felt such a fool, but the restaurant owner was very understanding **and found a table for us.** Then he phoned the other restaurant, which belonged to his brother-in-law, anyway!

Speaker 5
Last Saturday was very nearly a disaster. Some friends were visiting, so I booked us an Italian restaurant in town for an evening out. I also booked a taxi for us all, but the weather was so bad that the road at the bottom of the hill flooded, and the taxi couldn't get through for a long time. So, when it finally got us to the restaurant, we were very late indeed, and the restaurant had given our table to someone else. They were very apologetic, though, and **offered us a half-price takeaway** with a free bottle of wine, so **we went home with loads of food** and drink and had a lovely evening, anyway.

Speaking p98

1 Ask students to explain the reason for their choice. Relevant vocabulary (to elicit or pre-teach) includes: *ornate*, *luxurious*, *tablecloth*, *crystal*, *chandelier*, etc.

Key

Photo 1

2 Check that students understand the words in the box by getting them to match opposites: *boring/lively*; *value for money/overpriced*, etc. Where they can't find an opposite, get them to suggest one, e.g. *cramped/spacious*.

Encourage students to use the 'speculating' expressions modelled in exercise 1, e.g. *It looks …, I expect …, … possibly …* . Ask them to suggest other similar expressions. (*Maybe …, It could be …, The [big table] makes me think that …,* etc.)

Suggested answers

Photo 2
It looks like an informal place to eat, but not very lively. The food is probably quite basic, but good value for money.

Photo 3
It's looks as if it's popular with families with young children, so it's probably quite noisy. I expect it's very informal and good value for money.

Photo 4
It looks friendly and informal, and popular with young people and also quite lively and exciting. It could be a bit noisy. I don't expect the food is very dear.

Photo 5
It looks quite formal and popular with older people and professionals. It's probably quite dear.

3 Key

No. Ian's final suggestion is a Chinese takeaway and Andrea's is an Indian takeaway.

Tapescript 20

Ian Shall we eat out tonight?
Andrea Good idea. Where do you fancy going?
Ian Well, we haven't had a Chinese for a while.
Andrea I'm not that keen on Chinese food.
Ian I thought you liked it.
Andrea Not that much. What about a curry?
Ian No, I don't fancy an Indian. We could go to that little restaurant on Church St.
Andrea *Daisy's*? The service is terrible. Can't we go somewhere nicer?
Ian *The Ship*?

Andrea You must be joking. The food costs a fortune there. Let's try somewhere mid-range.
Ian What about *The Seven Bells*?
Andrea I haven't been there – have you? It looks very noisy. And I expect the food's a bit basic. I'd prefer somewhere quieter. How about that Italian place, *Gianni's*?
Ian *Gianni's* is OK but it isn't very lively.
Andrea Well, we're running out of options.
Ian Why don't we get a takeaway?
Andrea OK.
Ian } Chinese.
Andrea } Indian

4 Key

1 f   2 c   3 h   4 a   5 g   6 d   7 e   8 b

5 Suggested answers

See also the descriptions of the restaurants in the key to exercise 2 above.

The group is celebrating the end of their exams so is likely to be quite lively and noisy. The restaurant in 1 doesn't look as if it would welcome large groups of lively young people. It would also be too expensive and too formal. Number 2 isn't so formal, but the menu may be rather limited – lots of fast food, such as burgers, pizza and so on. The restaurant in 3 is probably not ideal as there are likely to be a lot of young children (though this may not bother everyone). It looks informal, friendly, lively and good value for money. The restaurant in 4 would probably be a good choice as it looks as if they cater for large groups. It looks good value for money and full of young people. The restaurant in 5 looks too formal and quiet, and not suitable for large groups of young people.

Optional activity

Get students to suggest a local restaurant (or a real restaurant that they know well) and explain the reasons for their choice.

6 Go through any vocabulary problems with the whole class at the end.

Use of English p100

1 Explain that *-less* is normally used to form a negative adjective when the positive form of the adjective is *-ful*. (Otherwise, the most common way of making an adjective negative is to add the prefixes *un-* or *in-*.)

Key

-less

2 You can check answers by playing 'suffix snap'. One pair reads out all the adjectives in their list. Other pairs shout 'Snap!' if they have the same word written down. Each pair gets a point for every word in their list that no other group has written down.

Suggested answers

sunny, hairy, rainy, funny, etc.
financial, national, traditional, etc.
breakable, reliable, acceptable, enjoyable, likable, etc.
dangerous, enormous, various, etc.
beautiful, wonderful, helpful, painful, faithful, powerful, etc.
homeless, endless, powerless, careless, thoughtless, etc.

3 Before doing the task, refer students to the **how to do it** box for *Word formation* on page 64.

Key

a thoughtful   e fanatical
b thoughtless   f drinkable
c rainy   g harmful
d homeless

4 Tell students to answer as many as they can without using a dictionary. Then get them to check in their dictionaries, either in pairs or as a whole class, to find the remaining answers.

Key

1 harmful   6 pleasurable
2 sugary   7 tiredness
3 moderation   8 laughter
4 meeting   9 unhealthy
5 opening   10 absolutely

5 **Key**

1, 2, 6, 9

Vocabulary p101

1 Explain to students that these are fixed expressions, which means that although both the words have a similar meaning, the order can't be reversed, i.e. we **don't** say *tired and sick*, *choose and pick*, etc.

Key

a 2 sick and tired
b 3 pick and choose
c 1 safe and sound
d 5 peace and quiet
e 4 bits and pieces

2 **Key**

a adjective + adjective
b verb + verb
c adjective + adjective
d noun + noun
e noun + noun

3 **Key**

a less   d then
b front   e downs
c later

4 Explain to students that most of the word pairs are much less formal than the underlined equivalents in sentences a–g and so they should use them only in informal writing and conversation.

Key

a I'm sick and tired
b Sooner or later
c safe and sound
d pick and choose
e more or less
f now and then
g bits and pieces

Writing p102

1 Discuss as a class. Start by eliciting examples of facilities, to ensure that students understand what's being discussed. You could also ask them to suggest facilities that the school doesn't have, but which they'd like to have.

2 **Key**

c

3 **Key**

a Disadvantages
b Conclusion
c Introduction
d Advantages

4 **Key**

a pros and cons
b convincing
c consider
d drawbacks
e in favour of
f aim
g on balance

Optional activity

Ask students to suggest other similar expressions for any of the categories a–g, e.g.

b powerful, persuasive
c assess
f objective
g after careful consideration, overall

5 **Key**

For the proposal:
a b e f

Against the proposal:
c d g h

6 Before students begin writing, explain that bullet points can be used in a report such as this as a helpful way of presenting a series of points clearly and keeping within a word limit, but that in other styles of writing (e.g. essays and formal letters), complete sentences with linking words are a better option.

There is an assessed authentic answer to this task on page 13 of the *Writing and Speaking Assessment Booklet.*

Review p104

1 **Key**

a tender
b crunchy
c bitter
d greasy
e salty

2 **Key**

a wonderful
b furious
c forgetful
d penniless
e suitable
f financial

3 **Key**

a safe and sound
b Wait and see
c sooner or later
d more or less
e give and take

4 **Key**

a will turn up sooner or
b had been more careful
c and tired of
d in favour of installing
e is too mild

5 **Key**

The **purpose** of this report is to **examine** the **pros** and **cons** of the proposal to buy more computers for the school.

The most **convincing** argument is that the computers are too slow for broadband Internet.

The only **drawback** seems to be that there would be less money to spend on books in the coming year.

On balance I think that the proposal is worth recommending.

Going to extremes 9

Lead in p105

1 Suggested answers

1 untidiness; laziness
2 shopping; wasting money on things that she doesn't really need.
3 never being on time

2 Check that students understand the vocabulary in a–e. Elicit or explain that the suffix *-holic* means 'addicted to' (e.g. *alcoholic*, *workaholic*). Also check: *terrible time-keeper* and *obsessively well organised*.

Key

1 e 2 d 3 c 4 a 5 b

Tapescript 21

Speaker 1
I like everything to be in the right place. I suppose the thing that I am most obsessive about is my music collection. Every so often I reorganise it. Sometimes I put the singers and groups in alphabetical order, other times I do it chronologically. And once or twice I've organised them into what type of music it is. Now that I've downloaded all my music onto my iPod and computer, I don't know what I'll do!

Speaker 2
My husband is really tidy and I can't stand it! He has all his shirts at one end of the rail and all his trousers at the other end. His shoes are lined up neatly at the bottom, brown on the left, black on the right. It's just too tidy and I long to mess it up. Instead I just throw my shoes into the wardrobe and leave my clothes in a pile. It makes me feel better!

Speaker 3
When I'm feeling depressed, or fed up, or if I've had an argument with somebody, I go out shopping. I'll spend maybe £50 on a nice pair of shoes or a dress. I don't really need them, but it makes me feel better. Or I'll go and have my hair cut. It never fails to cheer me up, but it's an expensive way to improve your mood.

Speaker 4
I'm never on time – for some reason I find it impossible to arrive early for anything. I leave it to the last minute to get ready so I'm always holding people up. And if there's something I don't want to do, or it's difficult, then I'll avoid doing it. Sometimes I don't open letters if they look like bills and just chuck them in a drawer. I only pay them when I get a reminder a couple of weeks later.

Speaker 5
I can never bring myself to throw anything away. I hate to throw things away because I always think they'll come in useful one day. Of course, the problem is that I never do use them again because I forget that I've kept them! I have boxes of stuff in the loft going back years, and I've really no idea what's in them. I must have a big clear-out one day.

3 For b, check that students are using the structures presented in the previous exercises: *I'm a … for* nouns and adjectives; *I can never…* (or *I'm always …-ing*) for verbs.

In c, typical structures should be:

I think it's extremely/not very   easy/hard   to learn to … /to stop … -ing   because …

Suggested answers

a
2a Always being late is generally a bad habit.
2b The disadvantage of this is that a lot of space is taken up with possessions that you don't really need. The justifications for not throwing things away are that they may come in useful one day and that we are too quick to throw away items that could still be used.
2c Being a shopaholic is generally bad and can become a serious addiction. People can get into thousands of pounds of debt because they can't stop buying things which they don't really need.
2d Being very untidy is generally a bad habit unless, perhaps, you live alone.
2e Being obsessively well organised is a fairly harmless habit and does have its advantages, as well-organised people are usually reliable, efficient and good to work with. On the other hand, this may become more important than anything else, which could be a bad thing.

c
It is fairly easy to teach new habits to children, but as we get older we find it more difficult to change our habits. Addictive habits such as smoking are often extremely difficult to give up.

Reading p106

1 Suggested answer

It depends to a large extent on your personality. Most people can experience excitement pursuing normal activities such as sports, socialising with friends, watching films, etc.

A minority of people find such ordinary experiences unsatisfying and are driven to ever riskier challenges in order to experience excitement.

2 Key

Lynne Cox (top) and Kanchana Ketkeaw (bottom).

3 Key

a   very many (= 'too many to count')
b   very small
c   difficult to stay or survive in/unwelcoming
d   very wild and violent
e   regular; unchanging
f   very important
g   having only one goal
h   so enjoyable that you can't do without it

4 Before doing the task, remind students about the how to do it box for *Multiple choice* on page 10.

Key

1   A   (l. 9–12)
2   D   (l. 25–27)
3   C   (l. 32–33)
4   B   (l. 38–44)
5   D   (l. 46–48)
6   B   He endured *extreme cold* (l. 51) and *extreme heat* (l. 53).
7   A   (l. 58–60)
8   C   (l. 66–67)

Optional activity

For homework, get students to write an essay or prepare a talk on 'A person I admire'.

Vocabulary p108

1 Key

a A   b P   c A   d A   e P   f A   g A   h A

2 Suggested answers

a   warm-hearted
broken-hearted
b   absent-minded
broad-minded
c   self-centred
self-disciplined
d   big-headed
hard-headed
(big-hearted and hard-hearted and also possible)

3 Suggested answers

a   warm-hearted: positive
broken-hearted: negative
b   absent-minded: negative
broad-minded: positive
c   self-centred: negative
self-disciplined: positive
d   big-headed: negative
hard-headed; neutral
(big-hearted: positive)
(hard-hearted: negative)

4 Suggested answers

a   **warm-hearted**: behaving in a friendly, generous and sympathetic way, for example, by befriending a new employee or student and making them feel welcome.
broken-hearted: being extremely upset by something, e.g. at the end of a relationship.
b   **absent-minded**: being forgetful, never knowing where you have put something.
broad-minded: being accepting of behaviour or opinions that are different from one's own.
c   **self-centred**: thinking about yourself and your own needs, rather than those of others.
self-disciplined: e.g. not putting things (especially unpleasant tasks) off, and getting them done in good time, rather than at the last minute.
d   **big-headed**: being arrogant, for example boasting about one's achievements (e.g. qualifications that one has gained).
hard-headed: being realistic and unafraid to take difficult decisions.
big-hearted: similar to **warm-hearted**
hard-hearted: being unkind and unsympathetic to others.

5 You can also ask students to describe themselves.

Grammar p108

1 Encourage students to answer as many questions as they can before they look at the Grammar Reference section on Relative clauses (p.171).

Key

a 1, 3
b 4, 6
c 4. See **Defining relative clauses**, note 3. If students included any of the other sentences, see **Non-defining relative clauses**, note 3.
d 1, 4. See **Defining relative clauses**, note 2.
e non-defining relative clause
f 4. See **Relative pronouns**, note 2.
g 8. See **Non-defining relative clauses**, note 5.

2 Key

a That's the man **who**'s going to buy our house.
b I gave my daughter twenty euros, **which** she spent immediately.
c I live in a village called South Milton, **which** is a mile from the sea.
d Where are the sausages **which** mum bought on Saturday?
e Daniel Craig, **who** also starred in the gangster film *Layer Cake*, plays James Bond in *Casino Royale*. Daniel Craig, **who** plays James Bond in *Casino Royale*, also starred in the gangster film *Layer Cake*.

3 The exercise has deliberately excluded *that* as one of the options, but students might still ask you where it could be used correctly. If they do, tell them that this will be covered in exercise 4b.

Key

a The shop **where** I usually get my groceries stays open till 10, **when** most other shops are shut.
b This chest of drawers, **which** I inherited from my grandmother, is 100 years old.
c Patricia is the girl **whose** car we borrowed to go to that Spanish restaurant **where** they do great paella.
d Near my house is a park **where** there are some trees **which** my daughter loves climbing.
e The tall man **who** is standing over there is the cousin of the man **who** I introduced you to last night.

4 Key

The <u>underlined</u> relative pronouns can be omitted. The ones in **bold** could be replaced with *that*.

a The shop where I usually get my groceries stays open till 10, when most other shops are shut.
b This chest of drawers, which I inherited from my grandmother, is 100 years old.
c Patricia is the girl whose car we borrowed to go to that Spanish restaurant where they do great paella.
d Near my house is a park where there are some trees **which** my daughter loves climbing.
e The tall man **who** is standing over there is the cousin of the man **who** I introduced you to last night.

5 Key

a He's going to retire at 50, **which** I find surprising. (See **Non-defining relative clauses**, note 5.)
b Elvis Presley, **who** was probably the most famous pop star ever, died in 1977. (See **Non-defining relative clauses**, note 2.)
c Pam Fisher, **whose** older brother is a doctor, has also decided to study medicine.
d I got a letter this morning from my uncle Algernon, who lives in Canada.
   (Without the comma, the sentence would mean that the speaker has more than one uncle Algernon.)
e The childminder **who/that** looks after our children is ill today.

Listening p110

2 For authentic exam practice you could give students 45 seconds only to read the sentences before listening.

The phrases in bold in the Tapescript show where the answers can be located.

Key

1 sure
2 a (small child)
3 his bedroom
4 set
5 cute
6 oldest
7 shelves
8 markets
9 burglaries
10 a couple of

P= Presenter   A= Alec

P   Hello, good evening. Welcome to another edition of '*The World's Greatest …*'. This evening we have in the studio a man with an overwhelming passion for … well, just about everything! Alec Gardiner must be the world's most obsessive collector. He collects key rings, matchboxes, cartoon characters, beer mats, the free toys from cereal packets, cake decorations – you name it, he seems to collect it. So let's meet Alec and find out why on earth he does it. Good evening, Alec. Welcome to the studio.

A   Thank you. It's a pleasure to be here.

P   As you can imagine, the question on everybody's lips must be – why do you do it? What's the point?

A   Well, I don't think I'm mad. I think I'm quite normal really. But to be honest, **I'm not sure that I can answer that question,** other than it gives me a lot of pleasure. **I have been collecting since I was a small child.**

P   Well, lots of children collect things …

A   Yes, but I suppose I've just never stopped! I was never bored as a child because there was always something new to collect. Then **I had to organise and arrange them in my bedroom.** I enjoyed that. I started with the small toys out of cereal packets, then football cards, toy cars, that sort of thing. And I've still got them! As I became older I became interested in more things and started collecting them as well. **The most pleasing thing is when I find the last object to complete a set of something.** That's really satisfying. It's so great to know that you have got absolutely *all* of them!

P   So what exactly have you got and where do you put them?

A   Well, **cartoon figures are my favourite because they are so cute and funny.** I've got about 15,000 of them. Mickey Mouse has to be my all-time favourite cartoon character, and **he's the oldest cartoon character as well, so there are more things to collect!** I have about 6,000 little models of Mickey Mouse …

P   6,000?

A   Yep, just under 6,000 of Mickey alone – from all over the world. You'd be amazed where Mickey turns up! I have thousands of other cartoon characters, too, especially Disney ones. That's my largest collection, simply because there are so many to collect.

P   And where are they?

A   **All in my living room. The walls are covered with little shelves.** I have a thousand key rings, as well, hanging on the walls. I have a lot of glass cabinets too. I've got 5,000 matchboxes in one of them, for example.

P   Wow! And how do you buy them?

A   Well, **there are collectors' markets and little antique shops,** of course. That was my main source before. But now I mostly buy on the Net – eBay for example. I'm a computer consultant, anyway, so I seem to spend most of my life online in front of the computer these days, whether it's work or pleasure. Anyway, **I don't like to leave the house for very long. Everything in there is precious, and I'm worried about burglaries.**

P   And how much do you think you spend?

A   Not sure. Oh, not much. Well, not for each individual thing, anyway. I suppose I must have spent thousands and thousands of pounds over the years. Although, **sometimes I have to spend a couple of hundred pounds to complete a set of something.**

P   A couple of hundred pounds for a Disney model?

A   Well, yes, but it's worth it to me.

P   So, what's next?

A   I'm trying to buy the house next door. I need more space.

P   You'll be collecting the whole street next!

A   That's an idea … !

P   Well, Alec, thank you very much for coming in to share your passion with us.

A   You're welcome.

3 Key

a bored	d amazed
b interested	e worried
c pleasing, satisfying	

The *-ed* form is used to say how people feel (or felt). The *-ing* form to describe whatever **causes** the feelings (thing or person).

4 Get pairs to report back to the whole class on their conversation, and check that they are using the correct form.

Speaking p111

1 Suggested answers

Photo 1: glass-topped table, sofa, cushions, armchair, stools, cat, windows.

Photo 2: chair, tables, armchair, fireplace, painting, candlesticks, ornaments, silver teapot, cups and saucers, curtains, carpet.

2 Check that students know the meaning of all the adjectives before they begin the activity. Get them to match opposites (e.g. *bright/dimly lit*; *bare/cluttered*) and give examples.

Suggested answers

Photo 1: bare, bright, clean, cold, open-plan, tidy
Photo 2: cluttered, cosy, dimly lit
Either room could be described as *comfortable*, *uncomfortable* or *relaxing* according to taste. Students will get the opportunity to discuss this in exercise 4.

3 Explain that students may not be able to use all the phrases to talk about these two photos, but they should take note of them as they may be useful for other Part 2 tasks.

Suggested answers

Similarities

The most obvious similarity is that both photos show living rooms.

You can see some furniture in both photos.

Differences

The biggest difference between the two photos is that photo 1 shows a bright and modern room, whereas photo 2 shows a dimly lit/dark and old-fashioned room.

While photo 1 shows a tidy and clean room, the photo 2 on the other hand shows a room that is rather untidy.

The rooms and furniture are completely different in the two photos.

4 Suggested answers

The room in the first photo is in a modern house or apartment. The windows are large and extend right along one wall, letting in lots of light. Through the window we can see some trees. There's a wooden floor with a patterned design. What furniture there is – a sofa, an armchair, some large cupboards, a glass-topped table and a couple of wooden stools – is modern and looks expensive. The colours are pale and there are no ornaments, pictures or photos on the walls. A grey cat is jumping off the table onto the floor.

The room in the second photo is in a much older, probably quite large, house. The ceiling is high, and decorative. The window on the right is tall, but the thick curtains do not let much light in. There's a very ornate fireplace, made perhaps of marble, with an old painting above it. On the table there are cups, saucers and a teapot.

5 Suggested answers

a

Photo 1: professional people who work in the arts, architecture or the media. Perhaps a single person or a childless couple.

Photo 2: people with a lot of money or who value tradition. Probably people who have inherited the house from previous generations.

b

Photo 1: They probably spend a lot of time at work and not a great deal of time at home, (although they have a cat, which will need feeding!). They might eat out a lot.

Photo 2: They might spend time looking after the house and grounds, though they are likely to employ some staff to help them. Perhaps they like traditional country pursuits such as hunting, fishing and shooting.

Use of English p112

1 Key

1	phrasal verbs	3	comparatives
2	relatives	4	passives

2 If students give different answers for some of the questions, get the whole class to decide which is right. You could do this anonymously by collecting in written answers first.

Key

a time I saw Harriet was
b 'll be interested
c must have been there
d won't put up with
e is too hot to
f was cancelled due to
g can't afford to

Vocabulary p113

1 Make sure that students answer as many as they can before looking in a dictionary.

Key

1	elbow	6	thigh
2	wrist	7	calf
3	waist	8	ankle
4	hip	9	shin
5	palm	10	heel

2 Suggested answers

a	eye	3
b	arm	1
c	leg	5
d	foot	6
e	tongue	7
f	hand	4
g	face	8
h	brains	2

Optional activity

Ask students if they can think of body idiom expressions with an equivalent meaning to the ones in exercise 2 in their own language, and say if the parts of the body used in the expression are the same as or different to the ones used in English.

Writing p114

1 Allow only a minute for this. Get students to say what specific words and expressions helped them.

Key

a

2 Key

formal – because it is a letter to a company

3 Explain to students that queries a and d are most important because if there aren't any places available on the dates specified, or if under-17s aren't allowed to take part, then it's unlikely that the person making the enquiries will make a booking. Queries b and f, on the other hand, are merely requests for additional information.

Key

Paragraph 1
1 c
2 e
Paragraph 2
3 a or d
4 d or a
Paragraph 3
5 b or f
6 f or b

4 Explain that these polite request forms are generally used in formal correspondence but they are not normally used in informal writing or conversation.

Key

Could you *please* let me know ... ? (d)
I'd be *grateful* if you could tell me ... ? (b)
I *wonder* if you could inform me ... ? (e)
Could you possibly give me some information about ... ? (a)
Could I *have* some details about ... ? (c)
Would it be possible to ... ? (f)

5 Suggested answers

a Could I/Would it be possible to
b Could you please/I wonder if you could/Could you possibly
c Could you possibly give me some information about/Could I have some details about
d I'd be grateful if you
e Could you please let me know/Could you possibly tell me
f I wonder/I'd be grateful

6 Key

a
single rooms? Paragraph 3
includes meals and hire of equipment? Paragraph 3
places available on 12–13/8? Paragraph 2
lower age limit? Paragraph 2

Suggested answers

b
Secondly, could you please let me know if there is a lower age limit?/I wonder if you could inform me if there is a lower age limit?

Would it be possible to have single rooms?/Thirdly, could you possibly give me some information about accommodation? Are there any single rooms available?

Finally, could you let me know if the cost includes meals and hire of equipment?/Finally, I'd be grateful if you could let me know if the cost includes meals and hire of equipment.

7 There is an assessed authentic answer to this task on page 14 of the *Writing and Speaking Assessment Booklet*.

Review p116

1 Key

a	minded	e	bad
b	tanned	f	self
c	broken	g	bald
d	headed		

2 Key

a	arm	e	tongue
b	foot	f	hand
c	brains	g	face
d	leg	h	eye

3 Key

1	amazing (a)	6	concerned (b)
2	terrifying (b)	7	convinced (a)
3	horrifying (a)	8	tired (b)
4	worried (c)	9	thrilled (a)
5	exhausting (c)		

All in the mind

Lead in p117

1 The Memory Test is in two parts, with part 2 in exercise 4. Memory is one of the themes of the unit, followed up in exercise 2, the quiz in 3, and the Reading section on page 118. To make the task more true to real life, tell students that they will hear the recording only once. For weaker classes, tell students in advance that they will hear the name, job, and home city of each speaker. The main information that they should remember is in bold in the tapescript.

Tapescript 23

1 Hi, my name's **John Logan**. I'm a **software engineer**. I live in **London**.

2 Hello, I'm **Becky Potter**. I'm a **nurse**, and I live in **New York**.

3 Hi, I'm **Kenny Jones**. I'm a **musician**, and I live in **Sydney**.

4 Hi. I'm **Susan Strong**. I'm a **waitress** and I live in **Los Angeles**.

5 Hello. I'm **Marc Brown**. I'm a **doctor**, and I live in **Toronto**.

6 Hello. My name's **Monica White**. I'm a **shop assistant** and I live in **Manchester**.

2 Suggested answers

a Phone numbers are generally easier to remember if they are not too long, if they have repeated numbers or a familiar pattern, or include numbers that represent something to the listener, e.g. similar to their own phone number/their birthday, etc.

b A tune is generally easier to remember if it is simple, involves a lot of repetition, has been heard several times, or is similar to another tune.

c Words which are similar to those in a student's own language may be easier to remember, as will ones with few syllables that follow simple spelling and/or pronunciation rules.

d Dances with simple, repeated steps, and that accompany a distinctive tune, should be easier to remember.

e These should be easier to remember if some comment was made at the time, or if they stood out for some reason, e.g. the colour, style, quality, similarity to the other person's own clothes, etc.

f The more complex the route to a place, the more difficult it would be to remember. Specific landmarks would make it easier, as would travelling in daylight rather than at night.

g A birthday near your own, or near or on a significant date should be easier to remember, or one with a pattern, e.g. 22/2.

3 Before looking at page 154, ask students to compare their answers and explain why they made the choices they did. After they have interpreted their scores, ask the class how many students have each learning style, *visual*, *auditory*, and *kinaesthetic*. Students discuss in pairs or as a whole class how knowing their learning style might be helpful.

Suggested answer

If you know your learning style you might be able to learn more quickly and effectively. For example, if you have a kinaesthetic learning style and want to learn a language, studying in a class with others would be the best option. Someone with an auditory learning style might do better with CDs, and prefer one-to-one lessons with a teacher. If you have a visual learning style you might be able to study alone from books, etc.

4 Key

a The person in photo 4.

b The other five names were Kenny Jones (1 on p.154, 3 on p.117), Monica White (2 on p.154, 6 on p.117), Marc Brown (3 on p.154, 5 on p.117), Susan Strong (5 on p.154, 4 on p.117) and Becky Potter (6 on p.154, 2 on p.117). Refer back to the Tapescript in exercise 1 for the other information they give about themselves.

Reading p118

1 The aim of this task is to show how difficult it is to make accurate calculations like these without the aid of instruments. The type of calculations in a–d are normally almost impossible for ordinary people to make. The reading text that follows is about savants, some of whom can perform such calculations easily.

Key

a Doors are normally about 800mm wide. It's impossible to judge to the nearest millimetre.

b It's impossible to guess the time to the nearest second.

c It was a Wednesday. It's very difficult and time-consuming to work this out, but not impossible.

d 35,004,816. This calculation is extremely difficult unless you are very good at mental arithmetic.

2 **Key**

a Ray Babbitt

b Kim Peek

c Allan Snyder

3 Before looking at the text, ask students to read the **how to do it** box for *Gapped texts* on page 94. For weaker classes, preteach some of the following words and expressions:

a home (1. 12) = a place where people who cannot care for themselves live and are cared for by others

feats (1. 49) = actions or pieces of work that need skill, strength, or courage

abstract (1. 51) = based on general ideas, not a particular real thing

acquire (1. 57) = to get or obtain something

Key

1 E Charlie and Ray have already been referred to in 1. 11. *For example* (1. 13) suggests that the missing sentence will refer to Ray's special abilities, and contrast them with his lack of life skills.

2 C The reference to Kim Peek's age in the previous and following sentence suggests that the missing sentence will also refer to his age.

3 A The examples of savants' special abilities in the sentences before and after the gap suggest that the missing sentence will contain an example of a specific ability.

4 D The reference to Tammet being *a good communicator* (1. 48) and to his explaining his own abilities (1. 49–51) are the main clues here.

5 G The topic in the preceding and following sentences is numbers. The use of the negative in the preceding sentence (*... do not involve*) fits with the contrasting word *Instead* at the beginning of G.

6 H *we all have these ... abilities ... but we lose them* (1. 53–55) contrasts with the savants who **don't** lose them.

7 B The reference to *Snyder* and to *experiments* confirm that this is the correct option.

Sentence F is not needed.

4 **Key**

a without hesitation (1. 2)

b with astonishing speed (1. 13–14)

c simultaneously (1. 25)

d fluently (1. 45)

e very occasionally (1. 57)

f temporarily (1. 65)

Vocabulary p120

1 **Key**

a 8 b 4 c 2 d 10 e 6 f 1 g 3 h 9 i 5
j 7

2 **Key**

a contemplate, doubt

b occurred, remind

c considered, analyse

d memorised, suspect

e recollect, comprehend

Grammar p120

1 **Key**

a comparatives: 1, 2, 5, 6, 7, 8
superlatives: 3, 4

2 **Suggested answers**

a My best friend doesn't drive as fast/quickly as I do.

b The weather is not as warm/hot in the autumn.

c Air tickets are getting cheaper and cheaper.

d In my opinion, this exercise is harder than it looks.

e This school is smaller than I remember it.

f Our local shops are not as close/near as we'd like them to be.

3 Suggested answers

a I think a footballer is probably richer than a ballerina. A ballerina is more graceful than a footballer. A ballerina isn't as athletic as a footballer.

b I think a big city is more exciting than a beach resort.
   A beach resort is certainly more enjoyable than a big city. A beach resort is also safer than a big city.

c Fast food isn't as healthy as seafood/lobster. Yes, but I think seafood/lobster is more expensive than fast food. Seafood/lobster isn't as tasty as fast food.

4 For weaker classes, explain to students that these sentences follow a regular structure. The first half starts with the comparative *The more* + adjective/adverb, followed by a noun and a verb. The second half repeats the same structure.

Suggested answers

a The richer people become, the meaner they get.

b The better I got to know him, the more I got to like him.

c The colder the weather becomes, the less I like going out.

d The more we use cars rather than public transport, the worse global warming will become.

e The more I study, the more tired I get.

Optional activity

Ask students to write sentences of their own using *The more ..., the more ...* . Suggest they write on specific themes (e.g. work, learning English, families).

5 Key

1 highest A   2 furthest C   3 most dangerous B
4 hardest A   5 largest A   6 most intelligent C

6 Use the examples to show how the questions are formed. Explain that the present perfect structure *you've ever (done)* is often used for asking about experiences. Tell students that it is also natural to answer using the past simple. Students should answer from their own experience. Encourage them to expand on their answers, e.g. explaining why, when, how this made them feel, etc.

Suggested answers

a What's the most dangerous thing you've ever done?

b What's the most/least interesting place you've ever visited?

c Who's the most/least attractive person you've ever met?

d What's the most/least expensive present you've ever bought?

e What's the most/least enjoyable film you've ever seen?

Listening p122

2 Encourage students to give examples from their own experience.

Suggested answers

People and places: People can behave differently from how they would in real life. They can say things that you hope or fear they might say but probably wouldn't in reality. Places that are far apart in real life can be very close to one another in a dream. Distances can be shorter or longer than in real life.

Sequence of events: Events can follow each other in an unnatural order or repeat themselves.

Feelings: In dreams you sometimes experience feelings that you suppress in real life, such as fear or unrealistic hope.

Time: Time can be distorted, with events and actions taking much longer or much less time than they would in real life.

3 Before listening, remind students about the **how to do it** box for *Multiple matching* on page 98. Make sure students understand the meaning of the word *weird* (= very strange or unusual and difficult to explain).

Key

Speaker 1	C
Speaker 2	E
Speaker 3	A
Speaker 4	F
Speaker 5	D

The extra letter is B.

Tapescript 24

Speaker 1

Other people always seem to dream about really weird, exciting things, but I don't. My dreams are boring. Even I think they're boring, and they're my dreams. For example, I might dream that I'm making a cup of tea, or a sandwich or something. Every detail is really clear. **Nothing strange or unusual happens.** Then I wake up and think, oh, it was just a dream. And that's it, really. I sometimes make up more interesting dreams, just to tell my friends.

Speaker 2

I usually dream about **things that have happened that day** – but they're slightly different. Things normally work out better in my dreams! So, for example, if I meet somebody at a party and talk to them for a while, **I'll probably dream about meeting them when I go to sleep that night.** Only, in my dream, I'll be much better at chatting to them – you know, really funny, making them laugh, being really interesting. I'm a much better, funnier, more interesting person in my dreams than I am in real life – unfortunately.

Speaker 3

I don't exactly have nightmares, but most of my dreams are, well, a little bit unpleasant. I mean, I usually feel anxious in my dreams because **things aren't going how I want them to go, and seem a bit out of control.** For example, I might dream that I'm getting ready to take an exam, but I can't find my pen or pencil. And then I look at the clock and see that the exam starts in five minutes, but I'm still at home, so I'm definitely going to be late … . **I know I'm messing things up,** but I can't help it. Stuff like that. I wake up with an anxious feeling in my stomach after one of those dreams.

Speaker 4

The odd thing is, I don't very often dream about people I know. **The people in my dreams are all new** – but I see their faces in a lot of detail. I mean, if I met somebody from my dream the next day, I would remember the face, even though I'd never really met them before – if you see what I mean. Mind you, if I came across somebody from my dream, I'd be terrified. So anyway, in my dreams, I act as though I know these people – sometimes they've got names. It's strange. Where do the faces come from? I've no idea.

Speaker 5

My dreams never really make sense. **They jump about, from one place to another, and they change suddenly.** So in my dream, I might be talking to a friend in my bedroom and the next moment, we're at the supermarket – and it isn't my friend, it's my brother. **One moment** I'm walking down the street, **the next moment** I'm flying over the sea. They move quickly, my dreams, like a weird film. Quite exciting really. I don't usually tell other people about them, though. There's nothing more boring than hearing about other people's dreams, is there? My brother is always going on about his dreams. It's so dull.

4 Speaker 1   make up
   Speaker 2   work out
   Speaker 3   messing … up
   Speaker 4   came across
   Speaker 5   going on

5 For weaker groups, give a list of verbs to match with the verb + preposition expressions: *spoil, meet, invent, talk, end*.

Key

Speaker 1 I sometimes *invent* more interesting dreams.

Speaker 2 Things normally *end* better in my dreams.

Speaker 3 I know I'm *spoiling* things, but I can't help it.

Speaker 4 If I *met* somebody from my dream, I'd be terrified.

Speaker 5 My brother is always *talking* (*a lot*) about his dreams.

Speaking p123

1 **Suggested answers**

a **heights**: the possibility of falling
   flying: not being in control; crashing
   open spaces: being exposed; unable to hide anywhere
   spiders: being bitten; dislike of their appearance
   thunderstorms: dislike of the sudden noise and light; being struck by lightning
   small spaces: feeling of being enclosed and unable to move; getting trapped
   public speaking: saying or doing something wrong or embarrassing in front of lots of people
   darkness: being unable to see what's around you
   germs and dirt: catching a disease
   water: drowning

b Photo 1 fear of heights, fear of open spaces
   Photo 2 fear of small spaces, fear of darkness, fear of water

2 Encourage students to suggest as many extra words as they can. For weaker classes, students could refer to bilingual dictionaries.

Key

Photo 1 a, f
Additional words: climb, vertical, grip, drop (n), hang, fall
Photo 2 b, c, d, e, g, h
Additional words: reef, underwater, swim, flippers,

oxygen, breathe

3 You could remind students of the phrases on page 111 for comparing photos.

Suggested answers

Photo 1 This activity would be enjoyable for people who like thrills and excitement. Reaching the top would also give a sense of achievement. However, it would be a nightmare for people who are afraid of heights or are anxious about things going wrong.

Photo 2 This activity would be enjoyable for people who like discovering unfamiliar worlds, such as the strange underwater life to be found on reefs. However, it would be a nightmare for people who are afraid of darkness or water, or being deep underground, or who dislike being in situations which carry a degree of risk.

Use of English p124

1 Before doing this exercise, tell students to read the information box on *Noun suffixes*. Use the examples of *dominate* > *domination* and *happy* > *happiness* to illustrate spelling changes. For more advanced groups, explain that stress patterns also change when suffixes are added, as in *domi̱nate* > *domina̱tion* and *si̱milar* > *simila̱rity*.

Key

a	punctuality	e	sensitivity
b	investigation	f	enjoyment
c	replacement	g	responsibility
d	politeness		

2 **Key**

a F b T c F

3 Explain that some answers might need a plural ending in addition to a suffix.

Key

1	belief	6	dedication
2	ability	7	achievements
3	important	8	greatest
4	different	9	highly
5	commitment	10	significant

Vocabulary p125

1 Students can check the meaning of any unknown expressions in a dictionary. Explain that they may find them under *mind* as a noun or under another word in the expression.

Key

a	verb	g	noun
b	verb	h	noun
c	verb	i	noun
d	noun	j	noun
e	noun	k	noun
f	verb	l	verb

2 **Suggested answers**

1 I'm bored out of my mind.
2 I hope you haven't changed your mind?
3 Would you mind not doing that while I'm working?
4 This film will take our mind(s) off our problems.

3 **Key**

a As she watched the plane land, her own first experience of air travel **sprang to mind**.
b I can't **make up my mind** which restaurant to go to this evening.
c **Would you mind** open**ing** the door for me?
d My dad **doesn't mind** giv**ing** us a lift into town.
e I don't want advice about my personal life. Please **mind your own business**.
f **Do you mind if** I give my friend your phone number?

Writing p126

1 Tell students to mark their answers by writing a–d next to the correct paragraphs.

Key

a fourth paragraph beginning *Here's my CV*
b third paragraph beginning *I have visited*
c second paragraph beginning *I am 22 years old*
d first paragraph beginning *I am writing*

2 Key

   a Dear Sir/Madam

   b Yours faithfully

3 You could ask students to find the inappropriately informal words or phrases in the letter before they look at the list of formal equivalents (a–g). They can use the list to help them if they can't find all seven straight away.

  Key

   a done (second paragraph)

   b Here's (fourth paragraph)

   c went to (third paragraph)

   d a few times (third paragraph)

   e getting a reply (fourth paragraph)

   f I want to (first paragraph)

   g lots of information about (fourth paragraph)

4 Key

   a 4 b 1 c 3 d 6 e 2 f 5

5 There is an assessed authentic answer to this task on page 15 of the *Writing and Speaking Assessment Booklet*.

Review p128

1 Key

   a John reminds me of a friend I had at school.

   b I doubt (that/if) we will win the World Cup.

   c I consider him (to be) very impolite.

   d For homework my daughter had to memorise a Shakespeare poem.

   e He's contemplating resigning and looking for another job.

   f We need to analyse the results of the experiment.

   g Can/Do you recollect exactly what he said?

   h The answer suddenly occurred to me while I was in the bath.

   i It's difficult to comprehend why she wants a divorce.

2 Key

   a astonishment   e illegal

   b discuss   f sadness

   c information   g careless

   d excite   h similarity

3 Key

   a discussion   e illegal

   b careless   f sadness

   c inform   g astonish

   d similarity   h excitement

4 Key

   1 invitations   6 commitments

   2 arrangement(s)   7 participants

   3 Psychologists   8 surprised

   4 difficulty   9 equally

   5 sincerely   10 sensible

Man and machine 11

Lead in p129

1 Ask pairs to report back on their conclusions when they have finished their discussion.

Suggested answers

a and b

1 record player: for playing vinyl records; replaced by audio cd and MP3 player
2 typewriter: for producing writing similar to print; replaced by computer
3 cassette recorder/player: for playing or recording sound and music on tape; replaced by CD player and MP3 player
4 video cassette: for recording and playing films and TV programmes; replaced by DVD and hard disk
5 floppy disk: for storing data that can be read by a computer; replaced by memory stick
6 walkman/personal stereo: for playing music while on the move, through headphones; replaced by MP3 player
7 fax machine: for sending and receiving documents in an electronic form; replaced by email and scans sent by computer; replaced by email
8 film camera: for taking photos on film; replaced by digital camera

Reading p130

1 You could expand this into a class discussion, and compare differences between girls' and boys' answers as well.

2 **Key**
b

3 Before looking at the text, remind students about the **how to do it** box for *Multiple Choice* on page 10. Encourage them to follow the stages when approaching these tasks.

Key

1 C (1. 7–9)
2 B (1. 10–13)
3 A (1. 20–23)
4 B (1. 36–39)
5 C (1. 59–62)
6 A (1. 63–65)
7 C (1. 72–75)
8 A (1. 79–80)

4 **Key**
a 3 b 5 c 1 d 6 e 2 f 4

Vocabulary p132

1 Elicit the meaning of the words in the box, and other vocabulary relating to mobile phones. Point out that *text* is used as a verb here, but that *send a text* is also possible; (*email* works in a similar way).

Key

1 text
2 Internet access
3 ringtones
4 battery life
5 wireless

Optional activity

Students can compare the features on each other's mobile phones or you could devise an activity based on a magazine or website that compares different phones.

2 Again, elicit or preteach relevant vocabulary. Point out the language structures in the mobile phone advertisement that are typically used in bullet-point format advertisements, e.g. initial verbs without subjects (*Chat to ...*; *Make and receive ...*; *Includes ...*) and descriptions without articles, *There is/are...*, *It has ...*, etc. (*Includes a high-resolution digital camera*; *There are Over 50 ringtones to choose from*).

Suggested answer

Mini-music 2

Download tracks and podcasts from your computer and play them on this great little MP3 player.

- store thousands of songs on the 40GB hard drive
- large colour screen makes it easy to use
- listen to your favourite music stations on the built-in radio
- includes comfortable headphones to make listening a pleasure

Grammar p132

1 Key

a *won* – second conditional

b *I'll burn* – first conditional

c *you press* – zero conditional

d *had known* – third conditional

2 Suggested answers

a What would you do/buy if you won the lottery?
What will you do/buy if you win the lottery?

b What film would you see if you went to the cinema this weekend?
What film will you see if you go to the cinema this weekend?

c Which places would you go to if you visited the UK this summer?
Which places will you go to if you visit the UK this summer?

d What kind of websites would you look at if you surfed the Internet at the weekend?
What kind of websites will you look at if you surf the Internet at the weekend?

e If you lost your mobile phone, would you buy the same model again?
If you lose your mobile phone, will you buy the same model again?

f What would you do if you didn't have any homework this evening?
What will you do if you don't have any homework this evening?

3

Get the pairs to report back by reading out some of their questions and answers to the whole class.

4 Key

a If I hadn't lost my old MP3 player, I wouldn't have bought a new one.

b If I'd known you liked opera, I'd have bought you a ticket.

c If I hadn't forgotten/If I'd remembered to shut the window, the burglar wouldn't have got in.

d If the computer hadn't been so expensive, Carl would have bought it.

e If I'd been able to find your number. I could have phoned you.

5 Key

a both

b 2

c both

d 3

6 Key

a We wouldn't have to walk to school ...

b ... if he hadn't been so rude to me.

c ... I would have read the manual.

d If you'd listened to the instructions ...

e I wouldn't be annoyed ...

f If the sea were warm(er) ...

7

Students can work in pairs or small groups, then compare answers as a class. If there is time, encourage the pairs to write two or three more sentences.

Suggested answers

a ... I'll check the weather forecast on the Internet.

b ... I had a computer at home.

c ... I'd have prepared more food.

d ... I didn't think they were so dangerous.

e ... I'd got every answer correct in the exam.

Listening p134

1 They were all invented by women, but let students confirm this from the Listening task in 2. For b, encourage students to come up with at least two reasons. These are also confirmed in the Listening.

2 Students' answers may vary; it is not always easy to predict the key words accurately until the information is heard in context. The purpose of this task is to make students read the questions carefully and to be aware of the type of information they are likely to hear.

3 The answers in bold in the Tapescript show where the answers can be located.

Key

1 B
2 B
3 C
4 A
5 C
6 B
7 A

Tapescript 25

Interviewer Welcome to 'Science Past and Present'. Today we have with us Dr Franklin, a professor of physics, who is going to talk to us about a subject dear to her heart – female inventors. Good morning, Dr Franklin. Can you tell us why you started researching female inventors?

Dr Franklin Yes. As you know, I teach physics, and young men far outnumber women in my department. So **I started to look for suitable role models as a way of encouraging more girls into the sciences,** especially physics and engineering. And I was very surprised by what I found. When I first started my research, my colleagues, both female and male, said, 'Oh, there aren't any women inventors.' But women are behind a much larger number of inventions than they are generally given credit for.

Interviewer Why is that, do you think?

Dr Franklin There are a few reasons. Until fairly recently in our society, women were not expected or required to be clever. In the past, traditional male and female roles did not encourage female education. **It was even considered unacceptable for a woman to be clever or educated. Therefore, women who did have ideas and who did invent things, often hid the fact.** Education was also costly and women often didn't own any money. **Actually, married women did not have legal rights to own** anything, **even their own ideas, for a very long time.** So, it was often the husband who was given the credit!

Interviewer So what did you find? When was the first female inventor?

Dr Franklin Well, the first time a patent was granted to a woman was in 1637. Between then and the beginning of the 20th century, there were 500 patents granted to women inventors.

Interviewer Is that a lot?

Dr Franklin Not at all, but it's a much bigger number than anyone would guess. **However, many more women inventors didn't even bother to apply for a patent. It wasn't considered ladylike!** For example, in 1842 Lady Ada Lovelace worked with Charles Babbage to invent the first computer. She was a brilliant mathematician, so she wrote the first computer programme. But she didn't patent it, because it wasn't socially acceptable for a woman of her class.

Interviewer Well, I didn't know that a woman made the first computer work! Can you tell us about some other women inventors?

Dr Franklin A lot of inventions by women were, unsurprisingly, designed to help with domestic tasks. For example, in 1886, an American woman, **Josephine Cochrane, patented her design for a dishwasher. She was fed up with the servants breaking her best dishes!** And in 1908, a German housewife called Melitta Bentz invented filters for coffee, because she was fed up with the mess that coffee grounds made. The Melitta coffee filter company still bears her name.

Interviewer And I know that you have found female inventors who have invented even more surprising things …

Dr Franklin Well, in 1902, **Mary Anderson, who came from hot and dry Alabama, was visiting New York. She was travelling by tram in very snowy weather.** She noticed how many times the tram driver had to stop the tram and get out to clear the snow off the windscreen. So, she invented the windscreen wiper! Soon they became a legal requirement for all transport. And then in 1908, a London woman, **Emily Canham, while being driven home in the dark, noticed the problem of blinding light from car headlights.** So, she divided the headlight into different parts. The top parts had different glass to shade the light, and only the bottom part was bright light. These were simple, practical solutions to potentially dangerous problems.

Interviewer How fascinating.

Dr Franklin Yes, things like the disposable nappy, by Marion Donovan, could be expected, but what about Stephanie Kwolek who invented the material for bullet-proof vests?

Interviewer Really? So, do you think that your female students will find these stories inspiring?

Dr Franklin I think *everybody* should be inspired by these clever people, men and women alike.

Interviewer I agree. Thank you, Dr Franklin.

Speaking p135

1 Key

penknife (Swiss army knife), watch, (pocket) calculator, remote control, iPod/MP3 player, (digital) camera

2 Tell students to write down their sentences (in order to check that they're using the conditional forms correctly). Then compare answers as a class.

Suggested answers

1 If we didn't have penknives, we wouldn't be able to carry around a small knife and all the other tools you get on these gadgets.

2 If we didn't have watches, we wouldn't be able to know immediately what time it was, unless we had another way of finding out the time such as a mobile phone screensaver.

3 If we didn't have calculators, we'd find it very difficult to do complicated mathematical problems in our heads, and it would take a long time to work them out on paper.

4 If we didn't have iPods/MP3 players, we'd have to start using portable CD players again, which are bigger and awkward to carry and cannot store music.

5 If we didn't have digital cameras, we'd have to start using film again. We wouldn't be able to take multiple shots of things and people and discard the ones that are no good.

3 Key

a TV remote control, digital camera, pocket calculator, watch.

b calculator and TV remote control

Tapescript 26

Female So which two gadgets do you think are the most useful?

Male That's a difficult one. I think the TV remote control is very useful …

Female Yes, so do I. But it is as useful as a digital camera?

Male Yes, digital cameras are useful. But most mobile phones include a digital camera nowadays, so in a way you don't really need a separate camera. If we didn't have TV remote controls, we'd have to get up and walk to the TV every time we wanted to change channels or adjust the volume.

Female OK, so shall we agree on the TV remote control?

Male Yes. What about the second gadget?

Female How about the pocket calculator?

Male Don't you think that a watch is more useful? I look at my watch all the time.

Female That may be true, but you can easily find out the time in all sorts of ways nowadays … on your mobile phone for example.

Male That's a good point, but I don't think the pocket calculator is a great invention.

Female Really? I use one all the time. I'm no good at mental arithmetic, so I'd be lost without a calculator.

Male Neither am I, so I agree with you there!

Female I think we need to make a decision. Calculator or watch?

Male All right. You've persuaded me. Let's go for the calculator.

Female So that's the calculator and the TV remote control.

Male Yes.

4 Practise saying the expressions with appropriate intonation, using the recorded conversation as a model, if necessary.

Explain to students that, in British English, disagreement is normally expressed indirectly. Direct expressions such as *You're (completely) wrong* or *I (absolutely) disagree* are generally only used in arguments between close friends or when people feel very strongly indeed about the subject under discussion.

Key

So do I.
Don't you think that ... ?
That may be true, but ...
That's a good point, but ...
I agree with you (there).

5 If there is time, get each pair to report back on their conclusions. Elicit appropriate reporting language, e.g. *We thought that ...* ; *We decided that ...* ; *We couldn't agree on ...* .

Suggested answers

(see also suggested answers to exercise 2)

penknife
Useful for cutting things and many knives have other tools such as scissors, nail-files, bottle openers, screwdrivers, saws, etc. Not many people carry them, so not many people would miss them.

watch
Useful for telling the time wherever you are. Some watches also have the date and other features such as a stop-watch. If we didn't have watches we'd need to carry around other timepieces, such as pocket watches, or use our mobiles.

(pocket) calculator
Useful for doing calculations. Without calculators we'd need to do the sums on paper or in our heads.

(TV) remote control
Useful for changing channels on the TV without getting up. See also the example for exercise 2 in the Student's Book.

MP3 player/iPod
Useful for listening to music while on the move. No need to carry around cassettes or CDs any more as you can store all of your music on the player. Can also be plugged into a stereo, so there's no need for a CD deck. Without them we'd have to rely on older technology, e.g. portable cassette and CD players.

digital camera
Useful for taking large numbers of photos. It's possible to delete poor shots and in many cases take them again until you are happy with the result. It's possible to load all the digital photos onto a computer, onto an iPod/MP3 player, and/or to print them.

6 Suggested answers

a Usually yes, but some gadgets have become very complicated to use (e.g. some DVD players, mobiles and computers) and are accompanied by thick manuals which are difficult to read and understand. We have come to rely heavily on gadgets, so when they go wrong it can be very disruptive to our lives.

b Good examples of unnecessary gadgets are things that do something electronically that could just as easily be done manually. Examples include electronic letter-openers, pencil-sharpeners and can-openers (although these items might be useful for people with disabilities).

c Computers are obviously very useful, sometimes indispensable, in the modern world. Like any tool, they are a problem when they go wrong and there is no other means of carrying out the task. However, few people would seriously suggest we go back to old-fashioned paper files, etc.

d Young boys and men in particular may spend a lot of time at their computers, either playing games or surfing the Internet. It is argued that all this solitary activity can lead to underdeveloped social skills.

Use of English p136

This section focuses on gapped prepositions in the open cloze, and encourages students to use a dictionary when practising this exam part.

1 Key

a	on	c	on
b	for		

2 Key

a	on	e	for
b	with	f	to
c	to	g	with
d	for		

3 Key

1	place	7	if
2	of	8	than
3	to	9	a/any
4	in	10	been
5	so	11	to
6	have	12	as

4 Key

a   4

b   3

c   2

Vocabulary p137

1 Key

a   Internet access, search engine

b   mobile phone, artificial intelligence, instant messaging

2 Key

a   search engine

b   instant messaging

c   mobile phone

d   Internet access

e   artificial intelligence

3   Explain to students that even native speakers and different dictionaries will often disagree about whether to use hyphens in some compound nouns. If they are not sure, they should probably not use them. The most important point for the exam is distinguishing between single-word and two-word compounds, as in this exercise.

Key

a keyboard	d computer screen
b website	e laptop
c battery life	f text message

Writing p138

1 Key

a, d, f

2   Explain that the first three expressions in the list have the same meaning.

Key

First paragraph: *Although*

Second paragraph: *but, despite the fact that*

Third paragraph: *However, but*

3   Explain that we normally use *the fact that* after *Despite ...* and *In spite of ...* . However, we **don't** use *the fact that* before a noun (e.g. *Despite the rain, I'm playing tennis this afternoon*) or before a gerund, which is a verb used like a noun, (e.g. *not receiving* in sentence a and *having written* in sentence f).

Key

a   Despite *or* In spite of

b   whereas *or* but

c   Despite the fact that *or* In spite of the fact that *or* Although *or* Even though

d   However

e   but

f   despite *or* in spite of

4 Suggested answers

Despite the fact that you claim your mobiles are reliable, the one you sent me didn't work.

The price quoted on the website is £100. However, I have since seen the same phone at a lower price.

I ordered a Mobifone 612 but you sent me a Mobifone 1100.

The price on the website is £100, whereas you charged me £110.

5   There is an assessed authentic answer to this task on page 16 of the *Writing and Speaking Assessment Booklet.*

Review p140

1 Key

a   wireless

b   instant messaging

c   text

d   ringtone

2 Key

a   5

b   6

c   8

d   1

e   7

f   2

g   4

h   3

3 Key

a   keyboard
b   battery life
c   artificial intelligence
d   laptop
e   website

4 Key

a   Although/Despite the fact that/In spite of the fact that
b   however
c   whereas/but/although
d   although/but
e   Despite/In spite of
f   However

5 Key

a   I'm writing to complain **about** a DVD player I bought from you.
b   You have **overcharged me** by £10.
c   I tried to **contact you** on a number of occasions, without success.
d   I would be most grateful **if** you would give me a full refund.
e   I look forward to **hearing** from you.

Make a difference 12

Lead in p141

1 Street crime: photo 3; vandalism: photo 4; homelessness: photo 5; graffiti: photo 1; begging: photo 2. Students may also say that photo 5 shows begging, but it is less overt than in photo 2. You could remind students of Speaking exercise 5 on page 51, about graffiti.

3 and 4 Students can do these in pairs, then compare answers as a class and have a wider discussion.

Reading p142

1 Key

Text A: photo 1
Text B: photo 3
Text C: photo 4
Text D: photo 2

2 Before looking at the text, remind students sbout the **how to do it** box for *Multiple matching* on page 22.

Key

  1 D (l. 73–74)
  2 A (l. 15–17)
  3 B (l. 38–39)
  4 B (l. 35)
  5 C (l. 55–56)
  6 C (l. 61–62)
  7 A (l. 28–29)
  8 C (l. 65–66)
  9 D (l. 74–75)
 10 D (l. 77)
 11 B (l. 41)
 12 A (l. 18–19)
 13 C (l. 66–67)
 14 D (l. 84–85)
 15 A (l. 16, 1. 24)

3 Key

a make   e bring

b have   f cause
c become   g earn
d raise

Vocabulary p144

1 With weaker students, use concept questions to check that they understand the expressions, e.g. *If you managed to do something, did you do it? (Yes.) Was it easy or difficult? (Difficult.)*, etc. For c, point out that there is no article, i.e. *to achieve success*, not *achieve a success*.

Key

a ambition   d manage
b target   e succeed
c achieve

2 Check that students also use the correct forms after the phrases in b, c and d (*achieve success **in**; succeed **in** … -ing; reach a target **of***). Encourage them to learn these as complete phrases or example sentences and to use a dictionary when they aren't sure.

Suggested answers

a The protestors **did not manage to change** the government's policy.
b Sophia Coppola **achieved success in** the film industry at a young age.
c Despite winning *Pop Idol*, she **did not succeed in making** a career in music.
d Last year, students from our school cycled around Britain to raise money for Oxfam, and **reached their target of** £60,000.

3 Ask students to say whether the word in each gap is a noun or an adjective. If they get b and d the wrong way round, explain that the opposite of *failure* is *success*, whereas an *achievement* is a specific success that has come about through effort by an individual or group of people.

Key

a realisation   d achievement
b success   e achievable
c successful

4 Check that students are using the phrases covered in the previous exercises and the appropriate tenses for each discussion point (e.g. *I succeeded in...; I (really) hope to ...; I managed to ... ; I haven't yet managed to ...*)

Grammar p144

1 Key

1 had (GR note 1)
2 let (GR note 6)
3 make (GR note 4)
4 got (GR note 2)
5 made (GR note 5)

2 When they have completed the task, get students to say which type of causative verb each sentence is:

- Things which we do not do ourselves but instead, pay or ask somebody else to do (GR note 1) Answers: a, b, d, e, f
- Unpleasant things which happen to us as a result of somebody else's actions (GR note 3) Answers: c and g

Key

a have, serviced   e have, delivered
b had, decorated   f have, developed
c having, taken   g have, stolen
d have, cut

3 Suggested answers

They've had the walls built.
They've had/they're having a garden made.
They've had the windows put in.
They've had the walls finished.
They've had the scaffolding removed.

4 Refer students to Grammar Reference notes 4 and 5 if they have problems in distinguishing the active and passive forms.

Key

a made, cry   d make, repeat
b was made to do   e makes, think
c were made to work f was made to wait

5 Make sure that each pair swaps roles halfway through the time you allow for this, so that each person takes a turn at asking and answering questions.

6 Suggested answers

a I would have my jacket cleaned./I would get the person who spilt the orange juice to pay the cleaning bill.
b I would let my friend borrow as much as I could afford./I would get him to tell me why he needed the money.
c I would let them do it./I would get the police to come and stop them.
d I would make the company give me my money back.
e I would let him come and get it./I would get him to go and play in the park instead.
f I would make her put the goods back./I would let her do it.

Listening p146

1 Encourage students to give reasons. They could discuss in pairs then widen into a class discussion.

2 The phrases in bold in the Tapescript show where the answers can be located.

Key

1 town hall
2 50,000 / fifty thousand
3 midnight
4 older people
5 shopping centre
6 (next) April
7 90 / ninety
8 Belgium ... France
9 safety
10 mobile phones

Reporter I'm with Jane Newton **outside the town hall** on a sunny but very cold morning, and I'm here to find out more about the council's new measures to reduce vandalism and other forms of crime and anti-social behaviour. Good morning, Jane.

Jane Newton Good morning.

Reporter Can I start by asking you to explain what the main problems are, in relation to crime – particularly crime committed by young people in our town.

Jane Newton Yes, of course. Well, vandalism is the main issue here. Damage to bus stops and public buildings in the town centre **costs the town more than £50,000 a year**. That's a lot of money.

Reporter Sure. So, what exactly is this new – and rather controversial – measure which you've decided to take?

Jane Newton Well, we've decided to install a device – called the Mosquito – which deters teenagers from hanging around in the town centre late at night – which is when **most of the vandalism takes place: between midnight and two o'clock**. The Mosquito gives out a loud, high-pitched noise. Teenagers find it really annoying, and basically, it makes them unwilling to hang around. The clever thing is that **older people can't hear it at all because the pitch of the sound is too high.** (Our hearing changes as we get older.) So it really does target the people who are causing the problems.

Reporter Where are you planning on installing it?

Jane Newton Well, wherever we need to. **The shopping centre is the first place we're going to try it out.** If that proves successful, we'll install further devices in other parts of the town centre – particularly in places where vandalism is a problem: bus stops, play areas, car parks … . **By next April, we plan to have ten of them.**

Reporter Now, how about some of the objections – some people have claimed that these devices discriminate against young people. I mean, what about young people who just happen to be in town late at night, who aren't doing anything wrong? This device harms them as much as it harms a teenager who is covering a wall with graffiti. How can that be fair? Aren't you treating all teenagers as criminals?

Jane Newton Look, we realise that not all teenagers are trouble-makers. But it's impossible to argue with the fact that **over 90 per cent of the vandalism in the town centre is done by teenagers**. And I want to make it clear that the Mosquito does not cause any physical harm. It's just an unpleasant noise.

Reporter But won't they just go somewhere else and commit the same crimes?

Jane Newton We don't think so. Other towns that have installed these devices have reported an overall reduction in crime as a result. It really does work!

Reporter It's true though, is it not, that **the Mosquito has actually been banned in some countries because it contravenes human rights. In Belgium, for example – and France too.**

Jane Newton I'm not sure about the exact legal situation in those countries. All I know is that in this country, it's perfectly legal to install the device.

Reporter Now, you say that the device causes no physical harm. But what about recent medical reports suggesting that the device could actually damage teenagers' hearing? Doesn't that worry you?

Jane Newton We are aware of that research – but we're also aware of other studies which show that this device causes no health problems. At the moment, **we're totally convinced of its safety.** Of course, if new evidence emerges, we'll look at it again.

Reporter Jane Newton, thank you very much. We've been discussing the Mosquito – a controversial device which is designed to deter teenagers from city centres by emitting a loud, high-pitched sound that's only audible to young people. Apparently, **some teenagers are now using the same sound as a ringtone for their mobile phones** – on the basis that if it rings in class, their teachers can't hear it! And with that, it's back to the studio.

Speaking p147

1 Elicit or preteach the meaning of the words and phrases in the box before students do the matching activity. Get them to identify opposites, e.g. *man-made/natural*; *in a social group/solitary*. Stronger students should know other relevant words and phrases, e.g. *in the wild*, *endangered*, *habitat*, etc.

Key

Photo 1: enclosure, man-made, protected, solitary
Photo 2: freedom, natural habitat, social group

2 Get students to underline the word or phrases in b, d, e and f which signal that it's an opinion/ speculation, rather than a factual observation. Ask stronger students if they can think of other examples of language that do the same thing, e.g. *possibly*, *maybe*, *It looks (to me) as if …* , etc.

Suggested answers

a factual
b opinion/speculation
c factual
d opinion/speculation
e opinion/speculation
f opinion/speculation
g factual

3 Encourage students to use the factual ideas from exercise 2 (a, c and g) and to add any other ideas of their own.

Use of English p148

1 The aim of this exercise is to show students how certain pairs of words can be synonyms in some contexts, but not in others. Encourage stronger students to try to answer as many as they can before looking at a dictionary, which they should use to check their answers.

Key

a	false/untrue	e	personal/private
b	false	f	personal
c	broad/wide	g	highest/tallest
d	broad	h	tall

2 **Key**

a True. (See paragraphs 5 and 6.)

b False. Her style of campaigning 'reaches people in a way that ... confrontation can't', but she does campaign actively.

c False. She has 'experience of the latest in green living' and has a 'long-standing commitment' to environmental living.

3 Before looking at the text, remind students about the **how to do it** box for *Multiple-choice cloze* on page 89.

Key

1 A 2 C 3 A 4 B 5 D 6 D 7 C 8 B 9 B
10 C 11 D 12 C

Vocabulary p149

1 Point out that in compound adjectives, the noun prefix comes first.

a 2 b 3 c 1 d 8 e 6 f 4 g 5 h 7

2 **Key**

a	meat-eating	e	record-breaking
b	Labour-saving	f	time-consuming
c	eye-catching	g	heart-warming
d	thirst-quenching	h	mouth-watering

3 **Key**

a Newspapers always put **attention-grabbing** headlines on the front page.

b He's always coming up with interesting **money-making** ideas.

c My uncle runs a **window-cleaning** company.

d In Nicaragua, Jinotega and Matagalpa are the largest **coffee-growing** areas.

e The **award-winning** film is being shown on TV tonight.

Writing p150

1 Explain to students that these sequencing words are very useful when presenting a series of arguments as part of a continuous piece of writing.

Key

2, 5, 4, 1, 3

Words that help: *First/Firstly, Secondly, Thirdly, To sum up*

2 **Key**

a 2, 3, 7

b 4, 5

c 1, 6, 8, 9

3 **Key**

1, 3, 5, 7, 8

4 For sentences a, b and e: Explain that *besides, as well as* and *in addition to* are normally followed by a verb in the *-ing* form.

For sentences c and d: Explain that when *Not only ...* is used at the beginning of a sentence, it's followed by an auxiliary verb then the subject (so we say *Not only are there ...* and not *Not only there are ...*) .

For sentence d: Get students to look up *moreover* and *not only* in a bilingual dictionary. Explain that *Moreover ...* is used to add new information to support something you've said previously, while *Not only ...* (followed by *... but also ...*) is used to say that something else is also true.

Key

a Besides banning cars from the centre, I'd have the roads resurfaced.

b Cars cause a lot of pollution as well as being noisy.

c Not only are there not enough buses, but they are old and dirty.

d Not only is the town hall old, it's also ugly.

e In addition to cleaning up the park I'd have a children's playground installed.

5 Point out to students that the advice in the **tip** box about using personal pronouns in articles is the opposite of what they should do in formal essays and reports, where personal pronouns should normally be avoided (see the **tip** box on page 67).

Key

All five paragraphs: Use of *I*.
Opening paragraph: '**We** would all like to …'
Final paragraph: 'if **you** visited Monkton, I'm sure
you'd agree …'

6 **For weaker students, brainstorm some of the vocabulary they might need, using each of the items in the box as a starting point, e.g.**

Air quality: *pollution, exhaust fumes, carbon levels,* etc.

7 **Suggested answers**
  a I'd have trees planted in the city centre.
  b I'd get the transport company to run more buses at busy times.
  c I'd make the air cleaner by banning big lorries from the city centre.
  d The government should make people recycle all their waste.
  e I wouldn't let them open supermarkets on out-of-town sites.

8 **There is an assessed authentic answer to this task on page 17 of the** *Writing and Speaking Assessment Booklet.*

Review p152

1 **Key**
  a succeeded   c managed
  b realised   d reaching

2 **Key**
  a achievement   d achievable
  b successfully   e unsuccessful
  c realisation

3 **Key**
  a There are three members of staff who speak Chinese where I work.
  b I've just bought a machine for making bread/ that makes bread.
  c A tarantula is a large spider that eats birds.
  d This magazine is full of ideas for saving money.
  e The goalkeeper was not really injured – it was just a tactic for wasting time.

4 **Key**
  1 A 2 C 3 D 4 B 5 C 6 B 7 D
  8 B 9 D 10 A

Unit and Progress Tests

Unit 1 test

1 Match adjectives a–e with nouns 1–5.

a bushy   1 eyes   ....
b full   2 skin   ....
c hazel   3 lips   ....
d hooked   4 eyebrows ....
e tanned   5 nose   ....

(5 marks)

2 For a–e choose the correct alternative in italics.

a As a boy, Phil had *pale/blond* hair, but now it's darker.
b Sonia has long, *straight/flat* hair down past her shoulders.
c Is it fashionable to have very *thin/narrow* eyebrows?
d I get sunburnt quickly because I have such *fair/clear* skin.
e The man in the photograph had *round/curly* red hair.

(5 marks)

3 Complete sentences a–f using the nouns below.

hand part row sense track word

a It's better to take .... in activities than just watch them.
b I'm not finding it easy to make .... of all these numbers.
c There's a lot to do, so could you lend me a .... ?
d Kate and Jack have had a big .... and aren't speaking to each other.
e I was working so hard that I completely lost .... of the time.
f I'm sure Micky will help because he gave me his ....

(6 marks)

4 Choose the correct form of the verbs in italics to complete the text.

I've decided I am (1) *getting/going to get* a new MP3 player on an Internet auction site. If I (2) *buy/'ll buy* it in the shops it (3) *costs/'ll cost* me a lot more, so as soon as I (4) *find/'ll find* one online that I like, I (5) *start/'ll start* watching it. I (6) *don't/won't* bid any money, though, until the auction (7) *is/will be* nearly finished. I (8) *am/'ll be* very disappointed if I don't win it!

(8 marks)

5 Choose the correct option, a, b or c, to complete each sentence.

1 I won't be at school next Tuesday because I _____ to the dentist's.
   a go   b 'm going   c 'll go
2 By the end of next year, they _____ building the new bridge.
   a finish   b are finishing   c will have finished
3 I'm sure that when I get home my parents _____ TV.
   a will watch   b will be watching   c are watching
4 By October, my girlfriend and I _____ out together for two years.
   a are going   b will have gone   c will have been going
5 Many scientists are convinced that in the future all the earth's ice _____ .
   a melts   b is going to melt   c is melting
6 My friends say the shop _____ me my money back for the clothes I bought.
   a won't give   b won't have been giving   c aren't giving
7 If you want me to, I _____ home with you.
   a 'll walk   b 'm walking   c 'm going to walk
8 We should set off for the station now, because the train _____ at 7.30.
   a is leaving   b leaves   c will have been leaving

(8 marks)

6 Choose the word, a or b, that best completes each sentence.

1 Sandra is a very _____ child and often starts crying.
   a sensitive   b sensible
2 Mr Hayes is a rather _____ man who doesn't agree with anyone.
   a sensible   b argumentative
3 Jill is a relaxed and _____ person who never upsets anyone.
   a loyal   b easy-going
4 George is a _____ friend who will support you whatever you do.
   a loyal   b bossy
5 Sally always uses her experience to find the best solution. She's very _____ .
   a sensible   b argumentative
6 That man is _____ . He's always telling everyone what to do.
   a easy-going   b bossy

(6 marks)

7 Use the word in capitals to form a word that completes each sentence a–f.

a The view from the top of the mountain was _____ .   SPECTACLE
b There was a(n) _____ explosion, but fortunately nobody was hurt.   POWER
c We went on holiday to a beautiful island with amazing _____ .   SCENE
d It was a wonderful _____ to complete all the Olympic buildings on time. ACHIEVE
e It's so _____ when you manage to do a job really well.   SATISFY
f My computer takes a long time to _____ songs from the Internet.   LOAD

(12 marks)

Total: / 50

Unit 2 test

1 Correct any incorrect prepositions in a–h.

a   The TV series is based in the book of the same name.

b   Penguins are slow on land but very good in swimming.

c   When watching wildlife, it helps to dress in dark clothes.

d   Your exam result will depend of how hard you study.

e   We arrived to our hotel just before it started snowing.

f   Climate change has had a big effect on the plants here.

g   The local fishermen's nets are all made with hand.

h   TV wildlife programmes seem to be popular all over the world.

(8 marks)

2 Replace the words in italics in a–e with one of these words and the correct preposition.

worried   risk   reason   full   hooked

a   My brother seems *addicted to* computer games.

b   In spring, these fields are *covered with* wild flowers.

c   Caroline is never *frightened of* walking home alone.

d   Some species of animal are *in danger of* disappearing.

e   We're not sure what the *cause of* the illness is.

(5 marks)

3 Complete sentences a–e with a suitable collective noun.

a   We saw a _____ of sheep on the hillside.

b   Mike gave Julie a _____ of flowers on her birthday.

c   There was a _____ of dogs on the street corner.

d   I always take a _____ of cards on holiday with me.

e   What a noise! It sounds like a _____ of elephants in the corridor!

(5 marks)

4 Match the groups of people with sentences a–f.

cast   team   staff   audience   crowd   crew

a   'We only lost the match because our best player was injured.'

b   'When the band come on the stage we all cheered.'

c   'We only get 20 days holiday a year in this company.'

d   'Our ship is often away at sea for three months at a time.'

e   'Hundreds of us waited outside the store for the sales to begin.'

f   'All of us enjoyed performing the last play at that theatre.'

(6 marks)

5 Match these words with definitions a–j.

lake   jungle   beach   lagoon   plain   valley   dune   coast   hedge   pond

   a a small area of fresh water, e.g. in a garden
   b a row of bushes along the edge of a garden
   c a hill of sand near a beach or in a desert
   d an area of salt water cut off from the sea
   e a large area of fresh water
   f part of a country near or next to the sea
   g a large area of flat land
   h low ground between hills or mountains
   i thick tropical forest
   j an area of sand next to the sea

(5 marks)

6 For 1–10 choose the correct alternatives in italics.

Many people enjoy (1) *walking/to walk* in the mountains at the weekend, but you risk (2) *to get/getting* into difficulties if you fail (3) *making/to make* the necessary preparations, such as checking the weather forecast. If conditions are likely to change quickly, put off (4) *to start/starting* your walk until later. I wouldn't recommend (5) *to set out/setting out* if heavy snow is forecast; imagine (6) *getting/to get* lost in a fierce snowstorm! If the situation is still not clear by the afternoon, it may be best to postpone (7) *to walk/walking* until the next day as you may not manage (8) *returning/to return* until after dark, which can be extremely dangerous. If you hope (9) *to go/going* up and down one of the taller mountains in one day, you should always try (10) *to reach/reaching* the top by midday, in order to have enough time to get down again in daylight.

(10 marks)

7 Complete sentences a–f using the correct form of the verb in brackets.

   a I remember .... (visit) a safari park when I was a child.
   b If your feet often get cold, try .... (wear) an extra pair of socks.
   c I'm tired so I'm to going to stop .... (have) a short rest.
   d Did you remember .... (switch off) the lights when you left?
   e I wish my sister would stop .... (take) things from my room.
   f After performing some new songs, the band went on .... (play) their best-known hits.

(6 marks)

8 Complete each conversation in a–e using one of these phrasal verbs in the correct form.

bring up   come across   come up to   keep up   take away

   a Q Why have you stopped running? The race isn't over yet.
        A I couldn't .... with the others; they're too fast for me.
   b Q How did you meet that boy?
        A He .... me and asked me to dance.
   c Q Didn't you live with your parents when you were a child?
        A No, they were abroad. I was .... here by my grandparents.
   d Q Where's my car? I left it here!
        A It was badly parked. I think it's been .... by the police.
   e Q Where did you find that lovely scarf?
        A I .... it in clothes section of the street market.

(5 marks)

Total: / 50

Unit 3 test

1 Complete the missing adjectives as in the example.

Example *attractive*   gorgeous

a   hot   ....

b   ....   ancient

c   cold   ....

d   ....   spotless

e   tired   ....

f   ....   starving

g   dirty   ....

h   ....   hideous

i   angry   ....

j   ....   hilarious

(5 marks)

2 For a–h choose the correct alternative in italics.

a   I heard an *absolutely/extremely* funny joke on the radio today.

b   That coat looks *extremely/completely* big on you.

c   Tickets for tonight's performance are *totally/very* expensive.

d   The weather this summer has been *completey/absolutely* awful.

e   I'm going to be *absolutely/really* busy again next week.

f   Two buildings were *quite/totally* destroyed by the explosion.

g   I'm *utterly/very* fed up with my neighbours complaining all the time.

h   The police are *absolutely/a bit* sure they know who robbed the bank.

(8 marks)

3 Rewrite sentences a–f using phrasal verbs with *put*.

a   Our local supermarket is going to increase the price of milk.

b   Why does that boy like to humiliate other children?

c   We have a big house so can accommodate six people.

d   Local people have provided the money for a new statue in the town centre.

e   Jane says her friends persuaded her to do it.

f   I simply can't tolerate that horrible noise any longer!

(6 marks)

4 Match sentence halves a–d with 1–4.

a   I don't know if Joe is putting   1   it down to a cat in the street.

b   He heard a strange noise, but he put   2   them across clearly to other people.

c   He has some good ideas but he can't put   3   it out and nobody was hurt.

d   It was a big fire, but the firefighters put   4   it on, or if he's really ill.

(4 marks)

5 Complete the phrasal verbs in a–f using each of these particles once.

across   away   down   in   off   through

a A recent rebellion was put _____ by the government.
b The risk of injury puts some people _____ playing rugby.
c My grandfather put _____ many years of hard work in that factory.
d Remind the children to put _____ their toys after they've played with them.
e The team don't know what they put their fans _____ when they play that badly.
f It's a complicated idea that I can't put _____ easily in words.
(6 marks)

6 Complete sentences a–f with the correct form of these verbs.

go   help   make   produce   take   view

a Everyone in the village _____ part in last year's carnival.
b Many people _____ him as a genius.
c Those shoes and trousers _____ together very well.
d The way he tells stories always _____ people laugh.
e The new traffic system didn't _____ the results we expected.
f This book can _____ people learn more quickly.
(6 marks)

7 For 1–10 choose the correct verb in italics.

One of the funniest stories I (1)*'ve heard/heard* recently was about a thief who
(2) *broke into/has broken into* an office block last year. He (3) *wanted/was wanting* to steal
an expensive new computer that the company (4) *bought/had bought*, so one night he
(5) *forced/was forcing* open a window and got in. The computer was quite heavy, and
as he (6) *has been lifting/was lifting* it through the window he (7) *dropped/was dropping*
his mobile phone. An hour later, the police arrived and discovered the phone, but soon
realised the thief (8) *stole/had stolen* that, too. Then they had a piece of luck, when a text
message came through saying 'Hurry up! I (9) *'ve waited/'ve been waiting* at the train
station for over an hour!'. When the thief eventually (10) *has arrived/arrived*, he was
arrested.
(10 marks)

8 Choose the correct form of the verb, a, b or c to complete each sentence.

1 When I got home, my parents _____ a new comedy show on TV.
   a watched   b were watching   c have been watching
2 How long _____ out with Richard?
   a have you gone   b are you going   c have you been going
3 Nobody laughed because they _____ that joke many times before.
   a heard   b had heard   c had been hearing
4 I think I _____ lots of mistakes in the exam.
   a made   b 've made   c 'd made
5 By the time Katy arrived, I _____ outside the cinema for half an hour.
   a stood   b 'd stood   c 'd been standing
(5 marks)

Total: / 50

Unit 4 test

1 For a–h, rearrange the letters to form a type of film, as in the example.

Example nationaim — animation

a raw

b starside

c newrest

d claimus

e unreadvet

f rororh

g mirec

h mycode

(4 marks)

2 Choose the correct alternative in italics to complete a–e.

a Some people found the film so *scary/slow* that they were too afraid to look.

b I couldn't stop laughing because the whole movie was so *funny/serious*.

c The story in the film was so *powerful/terrible* that I thought it was true.

d Nobody took the play too seriously: it was quite *light-hearted/gripping* really.

e It was such a *moving/boring* film that some of the audience were crying.

(5 marks)

3 Complete sentences a–j with *a/an*, *the* or no article.

a My father is in business and my mother is .... doctor.

b .... French are famous for their wonderful food.

c Patrick and Ryan are brothers. Ryan is .... taller one.

d Some people like .... rock but I prefer folk music.

e One day I want to travel through .... Africa.

f Louise learnt to play .... guitar when she was ten.

g Russia is the biggest country on .... earth.

h The most important thing to me is .... friendship.

i At .... Christmas we see all our relatives.

j After all that hard work I need to have .... rest.

(5 marks)

4 Match sentence halves a–e with 1–5.

a I took the wrong train and ended

b It wasn't easy to think

c In my teens, I used to hang

d Last night's concert started

e I completely forgot to shut

1 up a good name for our band.

2 around in the shopping centre.

3 down my computer last night.

4 up in a town 200 miles away.

5 off badly and then got worse.

(5 marks)

5 Find and correct ten mistakes with articles in the text below.

My family and I have decided that this summer we're not going abroad for
our holidays. Instead, we are going to spend all of the August in north of
England, in a small village by sea. We have rented small house in the Lake
District, which people say is most beautiful part of the country. Only problem,
I think, is a weather. Because of the mountains, and the winds that come
from Atlantic Ocean, there can be a lot of the rain. I just hope we don't end
up spending most of our time at the home.

(10 marks)

6 Replace the verbs in italics using phrasal verbs with *take*.

a I'd like to *start* Taekwondo, but there isn't a club near here.
b Several people were *deceived* by offers of cheap concert tickets.
c Many film actors *employ* an agent when they become big stars.
d The band really *became successful* after their tour of America.
e Manchester United were *easily beaten* again, this time 5–0 by Liverpool.

(5 marks)

7 Complete sentences a–f using the correct form of the verb in brackets.

a I _____ (wait) here for half an hour but the bus still hasn't arrived.
b Nigel _____ (always complain) about everything. He never stops.
c I _____ (not see) a film at the cinema for years.
d When my friend phoned me, I _____ (have) a shower.
e What _____ (you think) of that song they're playing at the moment?
f This time next year, I _____ (live) in Sydney, Australia!

(6 marks)

8 Complete the conversations in a–e using the correct form of these verbs.

sleep   play   fit   regret   have

a Q What's happening at the weekend?
   A Linda _____ a party on Friday night.
b Q What time did you come in last night?
   A At midnight. You _____ so you didn't hear me.
c Q When did you take up the piano?
   A I _____ it for more than five years.
d Q How does this shirt look on me?
   A It _____ you, I'm afraid. It's too small.
e Q Do you think I should spend all my money now?
   A You _____ it tomorrow if you do.

(10 marks)

Total: / 50

Unit 5 test

1 Match each of a–f with one of the prefixes below.

un in im il dis

a allow ....
b real ....
c logical ....
d sane ....
e possible ....
f practical ....

(3 marks)

2 Complete sentences a–h using these words with suitable prefixes.

active aware honest sympathetic grateful likely legal accurate

a Mark can be very .... sometimes. He didn't thank me for his present.
b In many countries, it's now .... to smoke in public places.
c I think your calculations are .... I make the total 250, not 245.
d I didn't see the red flag on the beach, so I was .... that swimming was dangerous.
e It was .... of Pamela to take those things from the shop without paying.
f Grant was a bully, so people were .... when he got into trouble.
g If my MP3 player is .... for more than a few minutes, it switches itself off.
h They might bring down the prices of those computers next year, but I think it's ....

(8 marks)

3 Match sentence halves a–d with 1–4.

a We don't have much time, so get
b It's a bad idea so we must speak
c We want your opinions, so speak
d Listen carefully so you don't get

1 your mind, please.
2 the wrong end of the stick.
3 to the point, please.
4 out against it.

(4 marks)

4 Choose the word or phrase that best completes each sentence a–f.

down behind out of into

a I like Matthew, so I'll try to talk him .... coming out with us.
b I know he's a big film star now, but he doesn't have to talk .... to everyone like that.
c Sheila's plan was to stay out all night, but fortunately I managed to talk her .... it.
d You should say it to her face, not talk .... her back while she's somewhere else.
e It's a pity you talked me .... buying a lottery ticket, because my favourite number won.
f I didn't want to spend the evening at the theatre, but my parents talked me .... going.

(6 marks)

5 Complete sentences a–f with suitable prepositions.

a People sometimes complain _____ losing money when shopping on the Internet.
b Whenever you buy something, you should insist _____ getting a receipt.
c I object _____ receiving emails from people I don't know.
d An actor has confessed _____ pretending to be the Prime Minister.
e Sophie begged her parents _____ some cash to buy a new mobile phone.
f Sammy is always boasting _____ how he was on TV once.

(6 marks)

6 For 1–10 choose the correct alternative in italics.

I was talking to Stacey last Monday and she told me she'd bought a new computer (1) *yesterday/the day before*. She said she (2) *was saving up/'d been saving up* for months to get it, so when she got it home and found it didn't work she was very upset. She phoned the shop and told the assistant that she (3) *can't/couldn't* switch it on, and asked him what he (4) *'s going to/was going to* do about it. He said that she (5) *had to/'d had to* take it back to the shop, but Stacey replied that it wasn't (6) *my/her* fault it was broken. She reminded him that she (7) *asked/'d asked* him at the time what (8) *had happened/would happen* if there were any problems, and he had said that they (9) *sent/would send* someone to repair it. In the end the shop assistant promised to sort it out (10) *this/that* afternoon, and by Monday evening it was working properly.

(10 marks)

7 Rewrite sentences a–e in reported speech.

a 'Who did you see at the café last night?'
She asked me _____
b 'I won't be late.'
He promised her _____
c 'They didn't tell me the truth.'
She complained _____
d 'You're making a big mistake.'
He told the police _____
e 'Do you want to phone home?'
They asked her _____

(5 marks)

8 Put the words and phrases below under the correct heading.

lie   forgery   legitimate   genuine   pretend   cheat   own up   truthful

honest	not honest
....	....
....	....
....	....
....	

(8 marks)

Total: / 50

Unit 6 test

1 Complete the idioms in a–f using these words.

dream   show   bad   scratch   easily   mind

  a After our passports were stolen, our holiday went from .... to worse.

  b After a year in Rome I spoke fluent Italian, which just goes to .... that the British can learn languages!

  c Jackie is rather shy, so talking in public doesn't come .... to her.

  d I knew I was going to be late and I needed a good excuse, but none came to ....

  e The village we stayed in was lovely, but I'm afraid the hotel didn't come up to ....

  f Sailing across the Caribbean with somebody I loved was a .... come true.

(6 marks)

2 For 1–10 choose the correct alternative in *italics*.

We reached the airport quite early, and went straight to the (1) *platform/check-in* to show our tickets and leave our (2) *hand luggage/suitcases* at the desk. The woman told us we would be (3) *boarding/picking up* the plane to New York in about two hours, so we went through (4) *passport control/ticket office* and then into the (5) *departure/customs* lounge. We had heard there was extremely bad weather in the eastern USA, and someone said the flight might be (6) *cancelled/taken away*, but we (7) *got into/got onto* the plane exactly on time. I put my bag into the overhead (8) *cabin/locker*, sat down and looked through the window. I was a little worried when I noticed there was ice on the (9) *wings/masts*, but the (10) *ticket inspector/flight attendant* explained that they would do something about that before we took off. I was very relieved!

(10 marks)

3 Match sentence halves a–f with 1–6.

  a At first the bus looked as though

  b We turned the heating off, in order that

  c Our room had a jacuzzi, as well as

  d The hotel was rather noisy, since

  e Travelling there was easy, whereas

  f Nobody seemed to know whether

  1 the train left at 6.30 or 9.30.

  2 the return trip took hours.

  3 it was so close to the airport.

  4 it was full, but we found a seat.

  5 the room didn't get too hot.

  6 a shower and a bath.

(6 marks)

4 The words in italics are in the wrong sentences. Decide which sentences they should be in.

  a Just before we left I realised both tyres on my *hovercraft* were flat.

  b We got off at the wrong stop and had to get back on the *plane*.

  c The waves were so high that I thought the *bus* was going to sink.

  d The *train* came down through the clouds and landed right on time.

  e A *ferry* is designed to travel smoothly just above the water.

  f We had a lovely meal in the buffet car of the *scooter*.

(6 marks)

5 Complete the dialogues in a–f using the correct form of *must* or *have to*.

a Q What do you _____ do to get a licence?

A First, you _____ have driving lessons.

b Q How much do you _____ pay to take the bus to college?

A You _____ pay anything. It's free for students.

c Q What kind of things _____ you do on the plane?

A Well, you _____ use your mobile phone, or smoke.

d Q Why does the flight attendant _____ count everyone?

A She _____ check that all the passengers are on board.

e Q Does the bus driver _____ stop here?

A No, he _____ stop if there's nobody waiting.

f Q Why _____ get up so early in the morning?

A Because I _____ get to work late.

(12 marks)

6 For 1–10 choose the modal verb, a or b, that best completes each sentence.

1 As the train came into the station, I _____ see him waiting there.

a can   b could

2 I think you _____ get more exercise and walk instead of driving.

a should   b must

3 I ran for the bus and in the end I _____ catch it.

a could   b managed to

4 You _____ go out in the car because there's no petrol in it.

a mustn't   b can't

5 I _____ hear the noise of the engines as the plane began to move.

a should   b could

6 Even when she was a small child, Nicola _____ swim very well.

a could   b managed to

7 At the airport, you _____ show your passport if they ask to see it.

a ought to   b must

8 People _____ always drive more slowly when go past schools.

a may   b should

9 All traffic _____ stop here when those red lights start flashing.

a must   b may

10 People _____ throw things out of car windows like that!

a couldn't   b shouldn't

(10 marks)

Total: / 50

Unit 7 test

1 Match sentence halves a–g with 1–7.

a My boyfriend's bus gets

b At the office, what gets

c My grandmother's getting

d This evening I want to get

e There's no way of getting

f I wish you'd stop getting

g We usually get

1 through two loaves of bread a week.

2 on now and needs a lot of help.

3 up to Chapter 6 in this book.

4 out of tidying your room.

5 here at six o'clock, I hope.

6 at me every time you see me.

7 me down is the boring work.

(7 marks)

2 Complete the dialogues in a–g replacing *get* with a different verb each time.

a Q Where did you get that hat?

A I .... it at the supermarket.

b Q Did you get here very early?

A Yes, I .... hours ago.

c Q I just can't get this pen to write properly.

A I can't .... this one work, either.

d Q You didn't get much of what she said, did you?

A No, I .... almost none of it.

e Q Do you think summer temperatures are getting higher?

A Yes, definitely. It's .... hotter ever year now.

f Q Do you think our daughter will get good results?

A Yes, I'm sure she will .... excellent marks.

g Q You're lucky. You never seem to get colds in the winter.

A Actually, I've been .... with one for the last two days.

(7 marks)

3 Rewrite sentences a–j in the passive.

a Somebody has sent me another message.

b They may have made a mistake.

c They've told him not to do that again.

d You can usually see something on the screen.

e They shouldn't allow things like that.

f Somebody must have seen the accident.

g They can't have sold the tickets already.

h Everyone thinks the computer was stolen.

i My penfriend sent me an online birthday card.

j That shop sold me a damaged CD.

(10 marks)

4 For 1–10 replace the formal verbs in italics with phrasal verbs.

Hi Sam,

As you know, I'm hoping to (1) *depart* on a trip round the world next week, but there's a problem. Last month I (2) *submitted* applications for visas to go to several countries, but one of them has been (3) *rejected*. I'm sure I (4) *completed* the form properly, and I thought it had just been (5) *delayed* for a while, but now I've (6) *discovered* I can't go there at all, because I (7) *omitted* some important information. If I enter without a visa, they might even (8) *imprison* me. Anyway, I've (9) *calculated* that if I go by a different route, it'll (10) *accelerate* my journey by about two days!

I hope all's well,

Chris

(10 marks)

5 For a–h put the words in the correct order to form passive sentences.

a   at   repaired   the   computer   moment   being   my   is

....

b   has   crime   for   arrested   the   been   someone

....

c   library   not   must   books   removed   from   be   the

....

d   been   a   taken   decision   have   yesterday   could

....

e   that   was   nobody   it   injured   thought   was

....

f   yet   the   not   received   have   message   been   might

....

g   away   believed   thief   have   the   to   is   got

....

h   message   was   her   by   he   a   text   sent

....

(16 marks)

Total: / 50

Unit 8 test

1 Correct the mistakes in sentences a–i.

a After a busy day, it's nice to get home to some peace and tired.

b I've put the food in the oven, so we'll have to wait and leave what it's like.

c Their parents were worried, but the children came home safe and quiet.

d Sooner or then, you're going to have to learn to cook for yourself.

e I'm sick and sound of having to wash all the dishes after every meal.

f I'm not that keen on pizza; I can take it or choose it.

g If you've not got much money, you can't pick and take where you live.

h Now and later, we go out for dinner instead of eating at home.

i Sharing a flat is much easier if everyone learns to give and see a bit.

(9 marks)

2 For a–j use the word in capitals to form a word that completes each sentence.

a For an evening of fun and .... , I'd recommend the new comedy club.   LAUGH

b The food at Jane's house was so .... that I asked her for more.   TASTE

c Are you .... sure that this is the right address?   ABSOLUTE

d It's terribly .... to eat food with so much sugar and fat in it.   HEALTH

e In winter, the restaurant's daytime .... hours are 11.30am to 3pm.   OPEN

f Karen isn't very .... of passing the exam.   HOPE

g Mick's car isn't very .... and it keeps breaking down.   RELY

h As long as you eat it in .... , food like that will do you no harm.   MODERATE

i The microwave isn't working properly; it's making a .... sound.   MYSTERY

j Drivers suffering from .... can be a danger on the roads.   TIRED

(10 marks)

3 For a–g choose the word, a, b or c, that best completes each sentence.

1 Children love ice-cream because it's so .... and cold.
   a bitter   b chewy   c sweet

2 Boiled rice on its own is a very .... meal.
   a rich   b plain   c crunchy

3 My curry was so .... that I drank four glasses of water.
   a spicy   b mild   c tasteless

4 I enjoyed the fried chicken. It made a very .... meal.
   a tasty   b stodgy   c greasy

5 His steak was so .... that he needed a sharp knife to cut it.
   a tender   b chewy   c rich

6 The coffee was rather .... so I put more sugar in.
   a sweet   b spicy   c bitter

7 Green olives can be quite .... , but I generally like their flavour.
   a fatty   b bitter   c crunchy

(7 marks)

4 Complete each of sentences a–h with one of these words or phrases.

friendly   formal   cramped   value for money   romantic   trendy   overpriced   noisy

a With music always playing and people talking very loudly, it's a .... café.
b The room was rather .... because the tables were too close together.
c The food there is .... It isn't very good and it costs a lot.
d At my local takeaway, the staff are .... and they always have time to talk to the customers.
e You have to wear a suit so it's rather .... , but it's not an expensive restaurant.
f Fruit and vegetables at the street market are good .... and much cheaper than in the supermarket.
g It's a .... restaurant, popular with TV stars and pop singers.
h We're going somewhere .... for dinner. I think he's going to ask me to marry him!
(8 marks)

5 Complete sentences a–h using *must (have)*, *might (have)* or *can't (have)* and the verb in brackets.

a It .... (be) Martin in this picture. He's much taller than that.
b There are a few dark clouds in the sky, so it .... (rain) soon.
c I .... (leave) my phone at the restaurant last night, but I'm not sure.
d Steve .... (spend) all his money already. I lent him 100 euros this morning.
e These shoes are enormous; Joe .... (have) very big feet!
f They .... (fix) the air-conditioning yesterday because it's working now.
g I don't know where Barbara is but I think she .... (go) home.
h They've put too many drinks on this bill. They .... (make) a mistake.
(8 marks)

6 Rewrite sentences a–h using modal verbs.

a I'm certain that's not Sarah's motorbike.

b It's possible the café will be closed by ten o'clock.

c That's definitely the best restaurant in town.

d I'm sure your brother ate all the chocolates.

e It's possible the waiter didn't write down your order.

f I'm certain you didn't see Maria out shopping.

g I'm sure you're feeling full after all that food!

h There's no possibility that they cooked this properly.

(8 marks)

Total: / 50

Unit 9 test

1 Match a–f with 1–6 to form compound adjectives that describe appearance.

a	brown	1	-haired
b	curly	2	tanned
c	long	3	-headed
d	sun	4	-eyed
e	rosy	5	-legged
f	bald	6	-cheeked

(6 marks)

2 Complete the compound adjectives in a–h using these words.

headed   minded   disciplined   centred   hearted

a   Mr Taylor is extremely self- _____ . He only ever thinks of himself.
b   Our grandmother is a warm- _____ person and we're all very fond of her.
c   Vicky has become so big- _____ since her band made that CD.
d   You have to be broad- _____ when you're meeting so many different kinds of people.
e   Alan was broken- _____ when somebody stole his new bicycle.
f   My uncle is really absent- _____ and sometimes forgets where he put things.
g   Successful business people are usually quite hard- _____ .
h   You need to have good ideas and be very self- _____ to write a book.

(8 marks)

3 Complete each of a–j with a word ending in *-ing* or *-ed* formed from the word in capitals.

a	The team were _____ after crossing the Arctic ice on foot.	EXHAUST
b	People can do some _____ things when they really want to.	AMAZE
c	I was so _____ after queuing outside the exhibition for two hours.	BORE
d	Going to the funfair with friends is a really _____ day out.	EXCITE
e	Could you stop that please? It's a very _____ noise.	ANNOY
f	It's quite _____ that there's still no news of the two explorers.	WORRY
g	Thanks for the invitation – I'll be _____ to go to your wedding.	THRILL
h	I was _____ about Rachel because she wasn't looking very well.	CONCERN
i	Jay was extremely _____ when he fell over while he was dancing.	EMBARRASS
j	Programmes about people doing extreme things can be _____ .	ENTERTAIN

(10 marks)

4 For a–j choose the correct alternative in italics to complete each sentence.

   a The explorer Amundsen, *which/who/that* was Norwegian, was the first person to reach the South Pole.

   b In Wales, *which/when/where* I was born, many people speak Welsh.

   c I've got a watch *what/that/whose* can send out an emergency signal.

   d Next Monday is the day *which/what/when* I start my new job.

   e Jamie is the boy *who/whose/which* parents were on TV last night.

   f In 2005, *where/which/when* I was 16, we climbed one of the highest mountains.

   g Jeff, *whose/who/which* favourite activity is snowboarding, is in the Alps right now.

   h Anne, *who/whose/what* is now married, used to go out with my brother.

   i The street *that/where/which* I live is very close to the sports centre.

   j This lake, *which/where/what* is 100 kilometres wide, freezes over in winter.

(10 marks)

5 For a–h, join the two sentences together, omitting the relative pronoun where possible.

   a This is the photo. I took it from the beach.

   b This castle is open to the public. It was built in the year 1275.

   c I once met a climber. His ambition was to reach the top of Everest.

   d Paris is our favourite city. We had our first holiday together there.

   e An hour ago the weather was lovely. The match started then.

   f My mother works at the local hospital. She is a doctor.

   g Those are the people. I was telling you about them earlier.

   h I'm looking for a shop. I want to buy a phone card.

(8 marks)

6 For a–h complete the dialogues with these parts of the body.

eye leg foot brains arm tongue hand face

   a Q Do you know that man's name?

      A Wait – I'm trying to remember. It's on the tip of my ....

   b Q It was really funny when the boss made that mistake!

      A Yes, it was. I couldn't keep a straight ....

   c Q I'm doing my history homework. Can you help me with some dates?

      A Yes, you can pick my .... if you like.

   d Q Are you coming out with us for the evening?

      A Well I shouldn't, but if you twist my .... I suppose I will.

   e Q Can you help me bring in the shopping?

      A Yes, I'll give you a .... in a moment.

   f Q I need to have a quick shower, but the food is nearly cooked.

      A Don't worry, I'll keep an .... on it for you.

   g Q I thought you said you were going to have all your hair cut off?

      A Not really – I was just pulling your ....

   h Q You mean you didn't want me to tell Pam you like her boyfriend?

      A No, I didn't. You've certainly put your .... in it there.

(8 marks)

Total: / 50

Unit 10 test

1 For a–h choose the word, a, b or c, that best completes each sentence.

1 I'm going to _____ all these details for future use.
  a occur   b remind   c memorise

2 I _____ whether we will arrive at the airport on time.
  a doubt   b consider   c suspect

3 It suddenly _____ to me that I had met her somewhere before.
  a recollected   b reminded   c occurred

4 I can't _____ why Keith did such a stupid thing.
  a comprehend   b suspect   c contemplate

5 We need to _____ the situation and then decide what to do.
  a doubt   b analyse   c memorise

6 That song _____ me of our holidays last summer.
  a reminds   b recollects   c contemplates

7 I _____ *Oasis* to be one of the greatest bands of the 20th century.
  a analyse   b suspect   c consider

8 I _____ going to that part of Ireland when I was a child.
  a recollect   b memorise   c comprehend

(8 marks)

2 Match sentence halves a–e with 1–5.

a This job isn't easy. Would you mind
b I really need some money and don't mind
c The stairs are still wet. Please mind
d I've left my phone at home. Do you mind
e No, I won't tell you my age. Please mind

1 working at weekends.
2 your step.
3 your own business!
4 helping me with it?
5 if I use yours?

(5 marks)

3 For a–j use the word in capitals to form a word that completes each sentence.

a To many people, _____ is more important than being rich.   HAPPY
b It is my _____ that the money was stolen last night.   BELIEVE
c I'm interested in the human mind, so I want to become a _____ .   PSYCHOLOGY
d There is no _____ to buy anything until you sign the papers.   COMMIT
e There is often a lot of _____ between members of the same family.   SIMILAR
f Our maths teacher is leaving, so the school needs to find a _____ .   REPLACE
g The police have _____ for making sure nobody gets hurt.   RESPONSIBLE
h There is always great _____ at the children's party.   EXCITE
i You need to show _____ to be a good doctor.   SENSITIVE
j There will be a full _____ into the causes of the accident.   INVESTIGATE

(10 marks)

4 Complete each sentence a–h using one of these words plus a suffix.

able achieve astonish discuss important inform popular punctual

a We had a .... with our teacher about what we learned on our school trip.
b Everyone understands the .... of getting a good education.
c I'd like some .... about trains to London, please.
d Possibly her greatest .... was winning the Olympic gold medal.
e Mark has a lot of .... in all subjects, but he doesn't work hard enough.
f Zoe was late for school again today. She must improve her ....
g To my .... , a spaceship came slowly down to earth and landed near me.
h Jack has been much friendlier recently, so his .... has increased a lot.

(8 marks)

5 For 1–11 choose the correct alternative in italics.

Many people believe that the (1) *better/best* way to buy goods is by Internet. They say it is (2) *more/far* easier than going to the shops, and that paying by credit card online is just as safe (3) *than/as* using it in a supermarket or department store. It is becoming (4) *most and most/more and more* popular, they claim, because the range of products is (5) *far/as* wider than in any shop, and often the prices are also the (6) *lower/lowest* anywhere. Although it is true that buying online is the (7) *faster/fastest* -growing kind of shopping, it may not be (8) *more/as* safe as people think. The more we shop over the Internet, the (9) *more/worse* the problem of criminals stealing our credit card details becomes. Also, it is (10) *far/very* more difficult to return goods to a seller on the other side of the world (11) *as/than* it is to take it back to your local shop.

(11 marks)

6 Complete each sentence a–h with a suitable word.

a A motorbike isn't usually as expensive to buy .... a car.
b I'm worse at singing .... I am at playing the piano.
c In South America, ... largest country is Brazil.
d The traffic in the city centre is .... worse and worse.
e After running 15 kilometres, I was feeling .... and more tired.
f I think badminton is more fun to play than tennis, but much .... interesting to watch.
g The .... time you spend studying, the better you will do in your exams.
h In Canada, the .... north you go, the colder the weather becomes.

(8 marks)

Total: / 50

Unit 11 test

1 Match sentence halves a–e with 1–5.

a	The TV judges awarded	1	the competition, I never thought I'd win.
b	It was difficult to hold	2	a breakthrough in treating malaria.
c	When I decided to enter	3	a conversation in such a noisy place.
d	After he had passed	4	Carla and Matt the prize for best dancers.
e	Scientists have made	5	his driving test, Jason bought a car.

(5 marks)

2 Complete each of sentences a–j with a suitable preposition.

a Our new apartment is quite similar _____ yours.

b I've checked your computer and there's nothing wrong _____ it.

c There is a ban _____ using electrical equipment while the plane takes off.

d I'm afraid this battery isn't compatible _____ your phone.

e There's no demand _____ video cassettes nowadays.

f My sister has applied _____ a place at university.

g It's easy to spend too much money _____ new clothes.

h Nowadays I rely _____ email to keep in touch with other people.

i The driver of the red car was responsible _____ causing the accident.

j Everyone in the class has made a contribution _____ our magazine.

(10 marks)

3 For 1–5 choose the correct alternative in *italics*.

Sometimes a laptop can be very useful, (1) *whereas/but* normally I prefer using my home computer. (2) *Although/Despite* my laptop is fairly new, it doesn't have as much memory as the PC and it isn't quite as easy to use. For instance, you use a mouse with the PC, (3) *even though/whereas* on my laptop I have to touch a pad with my finger. I don't find that easy, (4) *although/in spite of* the fact that I've been using it for months. (5) *However/Despite*, it's great to be able to take the laptop with me wherever I go!

(5 marks)

4 Match a–h with 1–8 to form compound nouns.

a	battery	1	engine
b	text	2	tones
c	search	3	board
d	key	4	site
e	computer	5	life
f	ring	6	intelligence
g	artificial	7	screen
h	web	8	message

(4 marks)

5 Rewrite each of sentences a–h using *if*.

a I can't vote because I'm not 18.

....

b I haven't got a credit card so I don't shop online.

....

c I didn't buy a new phone because I didn't have enough money.

....

d I don't know Janie's address so I can't send her an email.

....

e It was so cold last night that I didn't go out.

....

f I didn't talk to Bill because I didn't see him at the meeting.

....

g I was at the club yesterday so I don't feel like going there tonight.

....

h You're sleepy now because you went to bed so late.

....

(16 marks)

6 Complete each sentence a–j with the correct form of the verb in brackets.

a   If you give me your number, I .... (phone) you tomorrow.

b   How would you send emails if your computer .... (stop) working?

c   If I .... (not have) time to write that essay this afternoon, I'll do it tonight.

d   I would have gone to the cinema with you if you .... (ask) me.

e   If you .... (not press) 'delete', you wouldn't have lost all your data.

f   I .... (not feel) so tired every day if I could get up later in the morning.

g   If you'd bought your printer in the supermarket, it .... (cost) you less.

h   We might have missed the plane if we .... (leave) the house any later.

i   If I hadn't had an argument with my girlfriend, we .... (be) together now.

j   We wouldn't need to be waiting here if we .... (buy) tickets yesterday.

(10 marks)

Total: / 50

Unit 12 test

1 Use the words below to complete the compound adjectives in a–j.

English   eye   heart   labour   meat   money   mouth   record   thirst   time

a   I think the most _____-quenching drink is freshly made orange juice.

b   Joe's got a really _____-catching new bike. Everyone turns to look at it.

c   This year's winner crossed the line in a(n) _____-breaking time of 9.6 seconds.

d   The travel company are looking for a(n) _____- speaking tourist guide.

e   One _____-saving suggestion is to walk instead of paying to travel by bus.

f   Cats are _____-eating animals that often catch mice and birds.

g   The game's nearly over and the winning team are using _____-wasting tactics.

h   I recently saw a _____-warming film about a child and his pet rabbit.

i   Housework is much less tiring when you use _____-saving equipment.

j   There was a _____-watering smell from the kitchen as our food cooked.

(10 marks)

2 Match sentence halves a–e with 1–5.

a   The charity's aim is to raise

b   We are determined to bring

c   Small protests don't often make

d   Wasting public money can cause

e   Most people on this march have

1   front page news or TV headlines.

2   a strong dislike for the use of violence.

3   the problem to everybody's attention.

4   public awareness of the problem.

5   a scandal that harms the government.

(5 marks)

3 Complete sentences a–h using these words once each.

addition   besides   matters   more   sum   only   top   well

a   There's been a terrible storm. To make _____ worse, there's no electricity.

b   Protesters came from the capital as _____ as from other parts of the country.

c   I don't feel like going out tonight. What's _____, I don't have much money.

d   The new buildings are very tall. In _____, they are too close together.

e   _____ money, we also need voluntary workers to help rebuild the village.

f   More people now have cars. On _____ of that, they are using them more often.

g   Not _____ were many trees damaged by the fire, but lots of animals lost their natural habitat.

h   To _____ up, the situation is improving, but much more needs to be done.

(8 marks)

4 Complete each of a–f with a word formed from the word in capitals.

a We're pleased that we have at last dealt _____ with that problem. SUCCESS
b Visiting the Amazon rainforest was the _____ of a dream I'd always had. FULFIL
c I think reducing air pollution is _____, though not at all easy. ACHIEVE
d Local traffic is more _____ now that there are fewer lorries in the city centre. MANAGE
e Perhaps her greatest _____ was making people aware of green issues. ACHIEVE
f Cleaning the river was the _____ of an idea we'd had for 30 years. REALISE

(6 marks)

5 Complete the dialogues in a–e using the correct form of these verbs.

achieve   fulfil   manage   reach   succeed

a Q Do you think Linda will be successful in her career?
  A Yes, I'm sure she _____ a lot in the future.
b Q Were you able to get your work done on time?
  A Yes, I _____ to finish it on Friday afternoon.
c Q Do you think the protest march will make any difference?
  A Well, I don't think it _____ in changing the government's mind.
d Q Do you think Patrick will ever become a pilot?
  A Yes, I think one day he _____ his ambition.
e Q Have you saved all the money you need?
  A No, we _____ our target yet, but we will.

(5 marks)

6 Rewrite sentences a–h using the correct form of causative verbs *have* or *make*.

a Somebody's going to paint our house next week.
b I always laugh in situations like that.
c My suit needs to be cleaned before Monday.
d They have to stamp your passport for you here.
e I always think of her when I hear that song.
f Sally hasn't been to the hairdresser's for six months.
g My parents said I had to go to bed early.
h It's not worth repairing that old computer.

(16 marks)

Total: / 50

Progress test 1

Units 1–3

1 For questions 1–10, read the text below and decide which answer (A, B, C or D) best fits each gap. There is an example at the beginning (0).

This western region, lying next to the ocean, has some of the most beautiful (0) _____ in the entire country. Although there are some small villages along the (1) _____ , it is a long way to the nearest big town. No railways or motorways connect this region with the rest of the world, so it feels quite (2) _____ here. To the north, the huge White Mountains almost cut the region off from the flat (3) _____ of the interior. The only way through them is over a high pass and down a narrow river (4) _____ . This is a particularly beautiful area, with spectacular white (5) _____ on either side as streams tumble from the mountains high above. All around are dense (6) _____ of pine trees, covered in snow in winter, and eventually the river pours into a lovely blue (7) _____ , over a kilometre in width. From there to the sea there is a series of green (8) _____ , full of wild flowers in spring, and then a line of (9) _____ , built up over the centuries by the winds sweeping in from the ocean and across the sand. Behind these lies a small blue (10) _____ once part of the ocean and still filled with sea water.

Example 0 A view   B sight   Ⓒ scenery   D scene

1	A beach	B coast	C area	D shore
2	A isolated	B urban	C crowded	D cosmopolitan
3	A hills	B shores	C dunes	D plains
4	A beach	B gap	C valley	D slope
5	A tides	B waterfalls	C currents	D channels
6	A hedges	B bushes	C forests	D fences
7	A lake	B beach	C puddle	D pond
8	A lands	B grounds	C beaches	D fields
9	A peaks	B dunes	C deserts	D mountains
10	A bath	B pond	C lagoon	D river

(10 marks)

photocopiable © Oxford University Press

2 For questions 1–10, read the text below. Use the word given in capitals at the end of some of the lines to form a word that fits in the gap in the same line. There is an example at the beginning (0).

Example   0 classmates

My friends

My friend Emma goes to my school, and we are
(0) _classmates_ this year. She likes to do new and interesting   CLASS
things, as she's quite (1) .... , but she's also very   ADVENTURE
(2) .... because she doesn't take unnecessary risks. She's an SENSE
easy-going person and never gets (3) .... which is another   ARGUMENT
thing I like about her, and she's never (4) .... either. Ben is   BOSS
different. In fact, he's quite different from anyone else
I know. He's (5) .... in the way he dresses, and he never does   CONVENTION
what people tell him to do. He's (6) .... , but at the same time   REBEL
he has a lot of special skills and (7) .... For instance, he   ABLE
writes, draws and plays music with a lot of imagination, so he's
highly (8) .... He's also brilliant at telling jokes. Sometimes CREATE
I think he's so (9) .... that one day he might become a   HUMOUR
professional (10) .... !   COMEDY

(20 marks)

3 For questions 1–5, complete the second sentence so that it has a similar meaning to the first sentence, using the word given. Do not change the word given. You must use between two and five words, including the word given. Here is an example.

Example   My brother gave me this jumper.
              given
              I _was given this jumper by_ my brother.

1 I've never heard a joke as funny as that before.
   ever
   That is the .... heard.

2 I started to learn Chinese over a year ago.
   learning
   I .... over a year.

3 I last went abroad when I was twelve.
   been
   I .... I was twelve.

4 The rain was so heavy last night that we stayed in.
   heavily
   Last night .... that we stayed in.

5 The thieves got away before the police arrived.
   already
   By the time the police arrived, ... away.

(10 marks)

4 For 1–10 choose the correct form of the verb (a, b or c) to complete the sentence.

1 That suitcase looks very heavy. I _____ it if you like.
   a 'll carry   b carry   c 'm going to carry

2 We _____ in this village since 2006.
   a are living   b lived   c have been living

3 I _____ for hours when at last I found the entrance to the cave.
   a looked   b had been looking c had looked

4 I can't come out with you because I _____ some work this evening.
   a do   b 'll do   c 'm going to do

5 The concert _____ twenty minutes ago.
   a began   b has begun   c had begun

6 Everyone _____ by the time we got to the restaurant.
   a has already been eating b already ate   c was already eating

7 This time next week I _____ in the sea.
   a swim   b 'll be swimming   c 'm swimming

8 We'd better hurry because the plane _____ in two hours.
   a will take off   b takes off   c has taken off

9 We reached the cinema quite late, but fortunately the film _____ .
   a hadn't started   b didn't start   c hasn't started

10 By 2015, I _____ all my studies, I hope.
   a 've finished   b 'm finishing   c 'll have finished

(10 marks)

Total: / 50

photocopiable © Oxford University Press

Progress test 2

Units 4–6

1 For questions 1–10, read the text below and decide which answer (A, B, C or D) best fits each gap. There is an example at the beginning (0).

Example   0 A travel   (B) journey   C voyage   D flight

Our (0) _____ to Greece began at six in the morning, when my family and I set off from the house in our old car. We'd only gone a mile when we got a (1) _____ tyre, and after we'd fixed that we had to hurry to the airport. We (2) _____ to reach the check-in just before it closed, then went through to the departure lounge. Soon we were (3) _____ the plane, and looking forward to our week on an island in the sun. I had a window seat, but since I was directly above the (4) _____ I couldn't see much, so I asked the flight (5) _____ if I could move to another seat. She found me one nearer the front of the plane, and later on I had a wonderful (6) _____ of the snow-covered mountains as we crossed over the Austrian Alps. The weather became sunnier as we approached Greece, and our plane arrived right on (7) _____ at Athens airport. Half an hour after we landed, we (8) _____ the train for the centre of Athens, where we (9) _____ trains for the port of Piraeus. It wasn't long before we were on the waterfront. After a short wait we were on board our ferry and sailing out to sea. It was a lovely trip, and when finally we reached our destination, the holiday was a (10) _____ come true.

1	A flat	B level	C dead	D broken
2	A could	B managed	C able	D succeeded
3	A riding	B flying	C stepping	D boarding
4	A wing	B mast	C platform	D sail
5	A officer	B helper	C assistant	D attendant
6	A scene	B view	C sight	D scenery
7	A moment	B hour	C time	D minute
8	A got into	B got onto	C got up	D got over
9	A changed	B moved	C replaced	D exchanged
10	A plan	B hope	C thought	D dream

(10 marks)

2 For questions 1–10, read the text below. Use the word given in capitals at the end of some of the lines to form a word that fits in the gap in the same line. There is an example at the beginning (0).

Example   0 unaware

Serial TV

Few people nowadays can be (0) _unaware_ of the existence of   AWARE
'soaps', shown weekly or even (1) _____ . Some of them are so   DAY
(2) _____ that they are impossible to believe. The characters are REAL
nothing like ordinary people and the stories are often (3) _____ . PROBABLE
In fact, in my opinion most soaps give a totally (4) _____ picture ACCURATE
of modern society. Surely people in real life are not as (5) _____ , HONEST
or as (6) _____ to their friends, as these awful TV characters? It   LOYAL
seems (7) _____ to me that anywhere in this country there could   LIKELY
be so many (8) _____ people behaving so badly and doing so many CIVILISED
(9) _____ things. I cannot be the only person who wishes these   LEGAL
unpleasant programmes would (10) _____ from our television   APPEAR
screens forever.

(10 marks)

3 For questions 1–5, complete the second sentence so that it has a similar meaning to the first sentence, using the word given. Do not change the word given. You must use between two and five words, including the word given. Here is an example.

Example   My brother gave me this jumper.
             given
             I _was given this jumper by_ _____ my brother.

1   So that nobody could get in, the doors were locked.
    order
    The doors were locked _____ get in.

2   'I broke the cup,' Robert said.
    admitted
    Robert _____ broken the cup.

3   'Do you like my new phone?' said Julia.
    whether
    Julia asked me _____ new phone.

4   Do you think you can persuade Karen to come out with us?
    talk
    Do you think you can _____ out with us?

5   'Who did you meet yesterday?' said Frankie.
    met
    Frankie asked me who _____ before.

(10 marks)

photocopiable © Oxford University Press

4 For questions 1–10, read the text below and think of the word which best fits each gap. Use only one word in each gap. There is an example at the beginning (0).

Example 0 than

THE RISE OF THE CITIES

For the first time in history, there are now more people living in urban areas (0) _than_ in country areas. Whereas (1) _____ 1970 about 37% of the world's population lived in towns and cities, that figure was up to 47% by 2000. By 2030 it will probably (2) _____ risen to over 60%, so it looks as (3) _____ there will be five billion people living in urban areas within a couple of decades. Overall (4) _____ fastest increase has been in the poorer countries, as richer parts (5) _____ the world already had two-thirds of their people living in cities back in 1970. Europe and North America, as (6) _____ as Latin America, now have three-quarters of their citizens in urban areas. Just as the total urban population (7) _____ grown, so the number of extremely big cities has increased. In 1975 there were just five cities with over ten million inhabitants, but that figure has (8) _____ steadily increasing. A report published (9) _____ the United Nations predicts that by 2015 there will be 26 such cities, most of them (10) _____ Asia.

(20 marks)

Total: / 50

Progress test 3

Units 7–9

1 For questions 1–10, read the text below. Use the word given in capitals at the end of some of the lines to form a word that fits in the gap in the same line. There is an example at the beginning (0).

Example   0 interesting

Dinner for two

We went to a really (0) *interesting* little restaurant the other	INTEREST
night, just off the main square. It's a (1) _____ little place,	FRIEND
with soft music that makes you feel (2) _____ as soon as you	RELAX
sit down. It's decorated in a really (3) _____ way, and it's the	TASTE
perfect place for a (4) _____ evening out. The food isn't cheap,	ROMANCE
but it isn't (5) _____ either, which is just as well as I don't have	EXPENSE
much spare cash at the moment. To start with, I ordered the	
prawns in garlic, which were (6) _____ , while my friend had	AMAZE
smoked fish. It was a bit (7) _____ , but tasted great. Then I had	CHEW
(8) _____ chicken with vegetables, and my friend had what he	FRY
said was the (9) _____ curry he'd ever tasted. After that we both	SPICE
had ice-cream and then coffee, to finish an extremely	
(10) _____ meal.	PLEASE

(10 marks)

2 For questions 1–10, read the text below and think of the word which best fits each gap. Use only one word in each gap. There is an example at the beginning (0).

Example   0 were

Walkers rescued in mountains

Seven walkers, including six schoolchildren, (0) *were* last night rescued from a mountain in Wales. The children, (1) _____ are all aged between 13 and 15, were taking part in a school expedition when the area (2) _____ suddenly struck by a severe storm. All six (3) _____ reported to be in good health after (4) _____ flown to a nearby hospital by a rescue helicopter, which picked (5) _____ up from one of the highest peaks in the mountain range. (6) _____ is thought that the group were close to the top of the mountain when extremely heavy rain, (7) _____ had not been forecast, washed away the track they had taken on their way up. They then found shelter in a cave, (8) _____ they stayed for the next eight hours. While there, they are reported to (9) _____ used their mobile phones to contact the local emergency services and ask for help to (10) _____ sent.

(10 marks)

       photocopiable © Oxford University Press

3 For questions 1–10, read the text below and decide which answer (A, B, C or D) best fits each gap. There is an example at the beginning (0).

Example   0   A getting down   B getting out   C getting away   D getting on

Cooking on a camping holiday

One of the attractions of going on a camping holiday is the feeling of (0) .... from everyday city life, of finding peace and (1) .... in the countryside, but this also means thinking about how you are going to prepare meals while you are there. Before you (2) .... , check you have essentials such as saucepans and frying pans, cups, plates, knives, forks, spoons for everyone, and various bits and (3) .... such as scissors, a tin-opener and a sharp knife for cutting everything. Work out more or (4) .... how much food you will need to take with you, bearing in mind that being outside all day will make people hungry and they will probably (5) .... more food than usual. On the other (6) .... , if you take too much you'll have to carry a lot of weight everywhere, only to end up having to (7) .... half of it. One possibility is to cook a favourite meal – something (8) .... like a stew – seal it in a plastic bag, freeze it, and take it with you for your first evening meal in (9) .... you arrive late at the campsite. Then you just (10) .... it in a pan of water, and it'll be ready to eat in no time.

1 A silence	B calm	C rest	D quiet
2 A set off	B set up	C set to	D set for
3 A parts	B objects	C pieces	D items
4 A lower	B little	C fewer	D less
5 A get at	B get down	C get in	D get through
6 A side	B hand	C arm	D foot
7 A throw on	B throw off	C throw back	D throw away
8 A tasteful	B tasting	C tasty	D tasteless
9 A case	B event	C chance	D matter
10 A roast	B boil	C grill	D bake

(10 marks)

4 For questions 1–10, complete the second sentence so that it has a similar meaning to the first sentence, using the word given. Do not change the word given. You must use between two and five words, including the word given.

Example   It last rained here in February.
         since
         It _hasn't rained here since_ February.

1 Perhaps Jennifer went to school earlier than usual.
    might
    Jennifer _____ school earlier than usual.

2 Could you possibly help me with these suitcases?
    hand
    Could you possibly _____ with these suitcases?

3 John didn't realise that two men were following him.
    he
    John didn't realise that _____ two men.

4 I imagine the children are still playing in the park.
    must
    The children _____ in the park.

5 Everyone expects Sally to win the cooking competition.
    that
    It _____ win the cooking competition.

6 They believe the owner of the house is living abroad.
    be
    The owner of the house _____ abroad.

7 Mrs Hayes reprimanded her son for behaving badly.
    told
    Mrs Hayes _____ for behaving badly.

8 That man may be a thief so I suggest you watch him carefully.
    eye
    I suggest you _____ that man because he may be a thief.

9 The traffic delayed us for over an hour.
    held
    We _____ the traffic for over an hour.

10 People say the man was running when he fell.
    said
    The man _____ running when he fell.

(20 marks)

Total: **/ 50**

Progress test 4

Units 10–12

1 For questions 1–10, complete the second sentence so that it has a similar meaning to the first sentence, using the word given. Do not change the word given. You must use between two and five words, including the word given. Here is an example.

Example My brother gave me this jumper.
given
I _was given this jumper by_ my brother.

1 Please remember that the show does not finish until very late.
mind
Please .... the show does not finish until very late.

2 I couldn't fix the computer because I didn't have enough time.
if
I could .... I'd had enough time.

3 I think that boy looks like your brother.
reminds
That boy .... your brother.

4 My parents will be happy to let you stay here.
mind
My parents .... you stay here.

5 The reason I was late was that I missed the bus.
if
I wouldn't have been late .... the bus.

6 Last night I suddenly thought of a way of making some money.
occurred
A way of making some money .... last night.

7 The charity hasn't managed to raise enough money yet.
succeeded
The charity still .... enough money.

8 Although the weather was bad, we still went to the beach.
spite
We still went to the beach, ... weather.

9 My bike needs to be fixed before I go on holiday.
must
I .... before I go on holiday.

10 I would never have won without their help.
they
I would never have won .... me.

(20 marks)

2 For questions 1–10, read the text below and think of the word which best fits each gap. Use only one word in each gap. There is an example at the beginning (0).

Example   0 it

Writing by Internet

In recent times, the Internet has made (0) _it_ possible to communicate with other people in many different ways, not only by email (1) _____ also through instant messaging and in chat rooms. As (2) _____ as keeping in touch with friends, we may contact strangers, and in (3) _____ of the fact that we've never met them, politeness is still important. Even (4) _____ you are writing an electronic message, the rules are quite similar (5) _____ those for writing a letter by hand. If you were writing a letter by hand, for instance, you (6) _____ not write entire words or sentences in capital letters. Neither would you send the letter if you (7) _____ not checked it first for spelling and grammar mistakes. Shortened forms of words are becoming more and (8) _____ common in text messages, but not everyone is familiar (9) _____ the latest ones. So use full words (10) _____ you're not sure the person you're writing to will understand the short forms.

(10 marks)

3 For questions 1–10, read the text below. Use the word given in capitals at the end of some of the lines to form a word that fits in the gap in the same line. There is an example at the beginning (0).

Example   0 elder

MY BROTHER

Michael, my (0) ...*elder*.. brother, works as a doctor in a hospital	OLD
in Scotland. I always knew he would be (1) _____ , as I think he	SUCCESS
always realised the (2) _____ of studying hard. From quite an	IMPORTANT
early age he had a lot of (3) _____ to his work, and I remember	COMMIT
his great (4) _____ when he passed all his exams with 'A' grades.	EXCITE
Despite this, he still found plenty of time for (5) _____ of all the	ENJOY
things that children do, and his (6) _____ with other kids was	POPULAR
only partly due to the fact that he used to help them with their	
homework. He's lucky in that he's always had great (7) _____ in	ABLE
his studies or work, and also (8) _____ in his personal life.	HAPPY
Unfortunately, my (9) _____ have not been quite as good as his.	ACHIEVE
Sometimes I wish there were more (10) _____ between Michael	SIMILAR
and myself, although most of the time I'm glad I'm me, not him!	

(10 marks)

     photocopiable © Oxford University Press

4 For questions 1–10, read the text below and decide which answer (A, B, C or D) best fits each gap. There is an example at the beginning (0).

Example   0 A done (B) made   C got   D had

Reclaimed from the sea

A recent story that has (0) _____ front-page news in the UK is the plan to flood land on the east coast of England. Following (1) _____ with local people, the Royal Society for the Protection of Birds (RSPB) has announced that it (2) _____ to buy a large area of farmland and turn it into a wildlife reserve. The flat land has been farmed ever since the Dutch (3) _____ to build a wall around it 500 years ago, (4) _____ a single island where previously there had been five. Now the plan is to make gaps in this wall, (5) _____ the sea come back in to cover the land to a depth of 50 centimetres. This, according to the RSPB, will (6) _____ to the return of many kinds of birds, fish, wild plants and animals that used to live there before it was dried out. The scheme also aims to protect the English coast from the effects of climate (7) _____ , in particular flooding, as the sea level continues to (8) _____ . The RSPB hopes to (9) _____ public awareness of this problem by (10) _____ people to visit the area when the work has been completed.

1	A information	B comprehension	C participation	D discussion
2	A considers	B arranges	C intends	D commits
3	A succeeded	B achieved	C reached	D managed
4	A creating	B bringing	C doing	D setting
5	A getting	B letting	C forcing	D allowing
6	A lead	B cause	C produce	D happen
7	A alteration	B difference	C change	D replacement
8	A rise	B lift	C climb	D ascend
9	A remind	B raise	C recollect	D restore
10	A making	B having	C encouraging	D advertising

(10 marks)

Total: **/ 50**

Unit and Progress Tests Answer Key

Tests key

Unit 1

1 a 4 b 3 c 1 d 5 e 2

2 a blond
  b straight
  c thin
  d fair
  e curly

3 a part
  b sense
  c hand
  d row
  e track
  f word

4 1 going to get
  2 buy
  3 'll cost
  4 find
  5 'll start
  6 won't bid
  7 is
  8 'll be

5 1 b 2 c 3 b 4 c
  5 b 6 a 7 a 8 b

6 1 a 2 b 3 b 4 a 5 b 6 b

7 a spectacular
  b powerful
  c scenery
  d achievement
  e satisfying
  f download

Unit 2

1 a based on
  b good at
  c ✓
  d depend on
  e arrived at
  f ✓
  g by hand
  h ✓

2 a hooked on
  b full of
  c worried about
  d at risk of
  e reason for

3 a flock
  b bunch
  c pack
  d pack
  e herd

4 a team
  b audience
  c staff
  d crew
  e crowd
  f cast

5 a pond
  b hedge
  c dune
  d lagoon
  e lake
  f coast
  g plain
  h valley
  i jungle
  j beach

6 1 walking
  2 getting
  3 to make
  4 starting
  5 setting out
  6 getting
  7 walking
  8 to return
  9 to go
  10 to reach

7 a visiting
  b wearing
  c to have
  d to switch off
  e taking
  f to play

8 a keep up
  b came up to
  c brought up
  d taken away
  e came across

Unit 3

1 a boiling
  b old
  c freezing
  d clean
  e exhausted
  f hungry
  g filthy
  h ugly
  i furious
  j funny

2 a extremely
  b extremely
  c very
  d absolutely
  e really
  f totally
  g utterly
  h absolutely

3 a Our local supermarket is going to **put up** the price of milk.

    b Why does that boy like to **put down** other children?

    c We have a big house so can **put up** six people.

    d Local people have **put up** the money for a new statue in the town centre.

    e Jane says her friends **put her up to (doing) it.**

    f I simply can't **put up with** that horrible noise any longer!

4 a 4 b 1 c 2 d 3

5 a down
    b off
    c in
    d away
    e through
    f across

6 a took
    b view
    c go
    d makes
    e produce
    f help

7 1 've heard
    2 broke into
    3 wanted
    4 had bought
    5 forced
    6 was lifting
    7 dropped
    8 had stolen
    9 've been waiting
    10 arrived

8 1 b 2 c 3 b 4 b 5 c

Unit 4

1 a war
    b disaster
    c western
    d musical
    e adventure
    f horror
    g crime
    h comedy

2 a scary
    b funny
    c powerful
    d light-hearted
    e moving

3 a a
    b The
    c the
    d –
    e –
    f the
    g –
    h –
    i –
    j a

4 a 4 b 1 c 2 d 5 e 3

5 My family and I have decided that this summer we're not going abroad for our holidays. Instead, we are going to spend **all of August** in **the north** of England, in a small village by **the sea**. We have rented **a small house** in the Lake District, which people say is **the most beautiful** part of the country. **The only problem**, I think, is **the weather**. Because of the mountains, and the winds that come from **the Atlantic Ocean**, there can be a lot of **rain**. I just hope we don't end up spending most of our time at **home**.

6 a take up
    b taken in
    c take on
    d took off
    e taken apart

7 a 've/have been waiting
    b 's/is always complaining
    c haven't seen/have not seen
    d was having
    e do you think
    f 'll/will be living

8 a 's/is having
    b were sleeping
    c 've/have been playing
    d doesn't fit
    e 'll/will regret

Unit 5

1 a disallow
    b unreal
    c illogical
    d insane
    e impossible
    f impractical

2 a ungrateful
    b illegal
    c inaccurate
    d unaware
    e dishonest
    f unsympathetic
    g inactive
    h unlikely

3 a 3 b 4 c 1 d 2

4 a into
    b down
    c out of
    d behind
    e out of
    f into

5 a about
    b on
    c to
    d to
    e for
    f about

6 1 the day before
    2 'd been saving up
    3 couldn't
    4 was going to
    5 had to
    6 her
    7 'd asked
    8 would happen
    9 would send
    10 that

7 a who I'd seen at the café the night before.
  b that he wouldn't be late.
  c that they hadn't told her the truth.
  d that they were making a big mistake.
  e whether/if she wanted to phone home.

8 **honest:** legitimate, genuine, own up, truthful
  not honest: lie, forgery, pretend, cheat

Unit 6

1 a bad
  b show
  c easily
  d mind
  e scratch
  f dream

2 1 check-in
  2 suitcases
  3 boarding
  4 passport control
  5 departure
  6 cancelled
  7 got onto
  8 locker
  9 wings
  10 flight attendant

3 a 4 b 5 c 6 d 3 e 2 f 1

4 a scooter
  b bus/train
  c ferry
  d plane
  e hovercraft
  f train

5 a have to, have to
  b have to, don't have to
  c mustn't, mustn't
  d have to, has to
  e have to, doesn't have to
  f do you have to, mustn't

6 1 b 2 a 3 b 4 b 5 b
  6 a 7 b 8 b 9 a 10 b

Unit 7

1 a 5 b 7 c 2 d 3
  e 4 f 6 g 1

2 a bought
  b arrived
  c make
  d understood
  e becoming
  f achieve
  g suffering

3 a I've/I have been sent another message./Another message has been sent to me.
  b A mistake may have been made.
  c He's/He has been told not to do that again.
  d Something can usually be seen on the screen.
  e Things like that shouldn't be allowed.
  f The accident must have been seen.
  g The tickets can't have been sold already.
  h The computer's/computer is thought to have been stolen./It is/It's thought the computer was stolen.
  i I was sent an online birthday card by my penfriend./An online birthday card was sent to me by my penfriend.
  j I was sold a damaged CD by that shop./A damaged CD was sold to me by that shop.

4 1 set off
  2 sent in
  3 turned down
  4 filled in
  5 held up
  6 found out
  7 left out
  8 lock me up
  9 worked out
  10 speed up

5 a My computer is being repaired at the moment.
  b Someone has been arrested for the crime.
  c Books must not be removed from the library.
  d A decision could have been taken yesterday.
  e It was thought that nobody was injured.
  f The message might not have been received yet.
  g The thief is believed to have got away.
  h He was sent a text message by her.

Unit 8

1 a peace and quiet
  b wait and see
  c safe and sound
  d sooner or later
  e sick and tired
  f take it or leave it
  g pick and choose
  h now and then
  i give and take

2 a laughter
  b tasty
  c absolutely
  d unhealthy
  e opening
  f hopeful
  g reliable
  h moderation
  i mysterious
  j tiredness

3 1 c 2 b 3 a 4 a
  5 b 6 c 7 b

4 a noisy
  b cramped
  c overpriced
  d friendly
  e formal
  f value for money
  g trendy
  h romantic

5 a can't be
  b might rain
  c might have left
  d can't have spent
  e must have
  f must have fixed
  g might have gone
  h must have made

6 a That can't be Sarah's
    motorbike.
  b The café might be closed by
    ten o'clock.
  c That must be the best
    restaurant in town.
  d Your brother must have
    eaten all the chocolates.
  e The waiter might not have
    written down your order.
  f You can't have seen Maria
    out shopping.
  g You must be feeling full
    after all that food!
  h They can't have cooked this
    properly.

Unit 9

1 a 4 b 1 c 5 d 2 e 6 f 3
2 a centred
  b hearted
  c headed
  d minded
  e hearted
  f minded
  g headed
  h disciplined
3 a exhausted
  b amazing
  c bored
  d exciting
  e annoying
  f worrying
  g thrilled
  h concerned
  i embarrassed
  j entertaining

4 a who
  b where
  c that
  d when
  e whose
  f when
  g whose
  h who
  i where
  j which

5 a This is the photo I took from
    the beach.
  b This castle, which was built
    in the year 1275, is open to
    the public.
  c I once met a climber whose
    ambition was to reach the
    top of Everest.
  d Paris, where we had our
    first holiday together, is our
    favourite city./Paris, which
    is our favourite city, is where
    we had our first holiday
    together.
  e An hours ago, when the
    match started, the weather
    was lovely.
  f My mother, who is/who's a
    doctor, works at the local
    hospital./My mother, who
    works at the local hospital,
    is a doctor.
  g Those are the people I was
    telling you about earlier.
  h I'm looking for a shop where
    I can buy a phone card.

6 a tongue
  b face
  c brains
  d arm
  e hand
  f eye
  g leg
  h foot

Unit 10

1 1 c 2 a 3 c 4 a
  5 b 6 a 7 c 8 a
2 a 4 b 1 c 2 d 5 e 3
3 a happiness
  b belief
  c psychologist
  d commitment
  e similarity
  f replacement
  g responsibility
  h excitement
  i sensitivity
  j investigation
4 a discussion
  b importance
  c information
  d achievement
  e ability
  f punctuality
  g astonishment
  h popularity
5 1 best
  2 far
  3 as
  4 more and more
  5 far
  6 lowest
  7 fastest
  8 as
  9 worse
  10 far
  11 than
6 a as
  b than
  c the
  d getting/becoming
  e more
  f less
  g more
  h further

Unit 11

1 a 4   b 3   c 1   d 5   e 2

2 a to
b with
c on
d with
e for
f for
g on
h on
i for
j to

3 a but
b Although
c whereas
d in spite of
e However

4 a 5   b 8   c 1   d 3
e 7   f 2   g 6   h 4

5 a If I was/were 18, I could vote./I could vote if I was/were 18.
b If I had a credit card, I would shop online./I would shop online if I had a credit card.
c I would have bought a new phone if I'd had enough money./If I'd had enough money, I would have bought a new phone.
d If I knew Janie's address, I would send her an email./I would send Janie an email if I knew her address.
e If it hadn't been so cold last night, I would have gone out./I would have gone out if it hadn't been so cold last night.
f I would have talked to Bill if I had seen him at the meeting./If I had seen Bill at the meeting, I would have talked to him.
g If I hadn't been at the club yesterday, I'd feel like going there tonight./I'd feel like going to the club tonight if I hadn't been there yesterday.
h You wouldn't be sleepy now if you hadn't gone to bed so late./If you hadn't gone to bed so late, you wouldn't be sleepy now.

6 a 'll/will phone
b stopped
c don't have
d 'd asked/had asked
e hadn't pressed
f wouldn't feel
g would have/would've cost
h 'd/had left
i 'd/would be
j had bought

Unit 12

1 a thirst
b eye
c record
d English
e money
f meat
g time
h heart
i labour
j mouth

2 a 4   b 3   c 1   d 5   e 2

3 a matters
b well
c more
d addition
e Besides
f top
g only
h sum

4 a successfully
b fulfilment
c achievable
d manageable
e achievement
f realisation

5 a will/'ll achieve
b managed
c will succeed
d will fulfil
e haven't reached

6 a We're going to have our house painted next week.
b Situations like that always make me laugh.
c I need to have my suit cleaned before Monday.
d You have to have your passport stamped here.
e That song always makes me think of her.
f Sally hasn't had her hair cut for six months.
g My parents made me go to bed early.
h It's not worth having that old computer repaired.

Progress test 1

1 1 B 2 A 3 D 4 C 5 B
6 C 7 A 8 D 9 B 10 C

2 1 adventurous
2 sensible
3 argumentative
4 bossy
5 unconventional
6 rebellious
7 abilities
8 creative
9 humorous
10 comedian

3 1 funniest joke I've ever
2 have been/'ve been learning Chinese for
3 haven't/have not been abroad since
4 it rained/was raining so heavily
5 the thieves had already got

4 1 a 2 c 3 b 4 c 5 a
6 c 7 b 8 b 9 a 10 c

Progress test 2

1 1 A 2 B 3 D 4 A 5 D
6 B 7 C 8 B 9 A 10 D

2 1 daily
2 unrealistic
3 improbable
4 inaccurate
5 dishonest
6 disloyal
7 unlikely
8 uncivilised
9 illegal
10 disappear

3 1 in order that nobody could
2 admitted (that) he had
3 whether I liked her
4 talk Karen into coming
5 I'd/I had met the day

4 1 in
2 have
3 if
4 the
5 of
6 well
7 has
8 been
9 by
10 in

Progress test 3

1 1 friendly
2 relaxed
3 tasteful
4 romantic
5 expensive
6 amazing
7 chewy
8 fried
9 spiciest
10 pleasant/pleasing/ pleasurable

2 1 who
2 was
3 are/were
4 being
5 them
6 It
7 which
8 where
9 have
10 be

3 1 D 2 A 3 C 4 D 5 D
6 B 7 D 8 C 9 A 10 B

4 1 might have gone to
2 give me a hand
3 he was being followed by
4 must still be playing
5 is expected that Sally will
6 is believed to be living
7 told her son off
8 keep an eye on
9 were held up by
10 is said to have been

Progress test 4

1 1 bear in mind (that)
2 have fixed the computer if
3 reminds me of
4 won't/will not mind letting
5 if I hadn't/had not missed
6 suddenly occurred to me
7 hasn't/had not succeeded in raising
8 in spite of the bad
9 must have/get my bike fixed
10 if they hadn't/had not helped

2 1 but
2 well
3 spite
4 though/if
5 to
6 would
7 had
8 more
9 with
10 if

3 1 successful
2 importance
3 commitment
4 excitement
5 enjoyment
6 popularity
7 ability
8 happiness
9 achievements
10 similarity/similarities

4 1 D 2 C 3 D 4 A 5 B
6 A 7 C 8 A 9 B 10 C

Answer Sheets

UNIVERSITY *of* CAMBRIDGE
ESOL Examinations

Do not write in this box

SAMPLE

Candidate Name
If not already printed, write name in CAPITALS and complete the Candidate No. grid (in pencil).

Candidate Signature

Examination Title

Centre

Supervisor:
If the candidate is ABSENT or has WITHDRAWN shade here

Centre No.

Candidate No.

Examination Details

0	0	0	0
1	1	1	1
2	2	2	2
3	3	3	3
4	4	4	4
5	5	5	5
6	6	6	6
7	7	7	7
8	8	8	8
9	9	9	9

Candidate Answer Sheet

Instructions

Use a PENCIL (B or HB).

Mark ONE letter for each question.

For example, if you think B is the right answer to the question, mark your answer sheet like this:

0 A B C D E F G H

Rub out any answer you wish to change using an eraser.

1	A B C D E F G H	21	A B C D E F G H
2	A B C D E F G H	22	A B C D E F G H
3	A B C D E F G H	23	A B C D E F G H
4	A B C D E F G H	24	A B C D E F G H
5	A B C D E F G H	25	A B C D E F G H
6	A B C D E F G H	26	A B C D E F G H
7	A B C D E F G H	27	A B C D E F G H
8	A B C D E F G H	28	A B C D E F G H
9	A B C D E F G H	29	A B C D E F G H
10	A B C D E F G H	30	A B C D E F G H
11	A B C D E F G H	31	A B C D E F G H
12	A B C D E F G H	32	A B C D E F G H
13	A B C D E F G H	33	A B C D E F G H
14	A B C D E F G H	34	A B C D E F G H
15	A B C D E F G H	35	A B C D E F G H
16	A B C D E F G H	36	A B C D E F G H
17	A B C D E F G H	37	A B C D E F G H
18	A B C D E F G H	38	A B C D E F G H
19	A B C D E F G H	39	A B C D E F G H
20	A B C D E F G H	40	A B C D E F G H

A-H 40 CAS

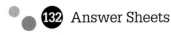

denote Print Limited 0121 520 5100

DP594/300

Do not write in this box

Candidate Name
If not already printed, write name
in CAPITALS and complete the
Candidate No. grid (in pencil).

Candidate Signature

SAMPLE

Examination Title

Centre

Supervisor:

If the candidate is ABSENT or has WITHDRAWN shade here ▭

Centre No.

Candidate No.

Examination
Details

0	0	0	0
1	1	1	1
2	2	2	2
3	3	3	3
4	4	4	4
5	5	5	5
6	6	6	6
7	7	7	7
8	8	8	8
9	9	9	9

Candidate Answer Sheet

Instructions

Use a PENCIL (B or HB). Rub out any answer you wish to change using an eraser.

Part 1: Mark ONE letter for each question.

For example, if you think **B** is the right
answer to the question, mark your
answer sheet like this:

0 | A | B | C | D

Parts 2, 3 and **4:** Write your answer clearly
in CAPITAL LETTERS.

For Parts 2 and 3 write one letter
in each box. For example:

0 | EXAMPLE

Part 1

1	A	B	C	D
2	A	B	C	D
3	A	B	C	D
4	A	B	C	D
5	A	B	C	D
6	A	B	C	D
7	A	B	C	D
8	A	B	C	D
9	A	B	C	D
10	A	B	C	D
11	A	B	C	D
12	A	B	C	D

Part 2

Do not write
below here

13		13 1 0 u
14		14 1 0 u
15		15 1 0 u
16		16 1 0 u
17		17 1 0 u
18		18 1 0 u
19		19 1 0 u
20		20 1 0 u
21		21 1 0 u
22		22 1 0 u
23		23 1 0 u
24		24 1 0 u

Continues over ➡

DP596/305

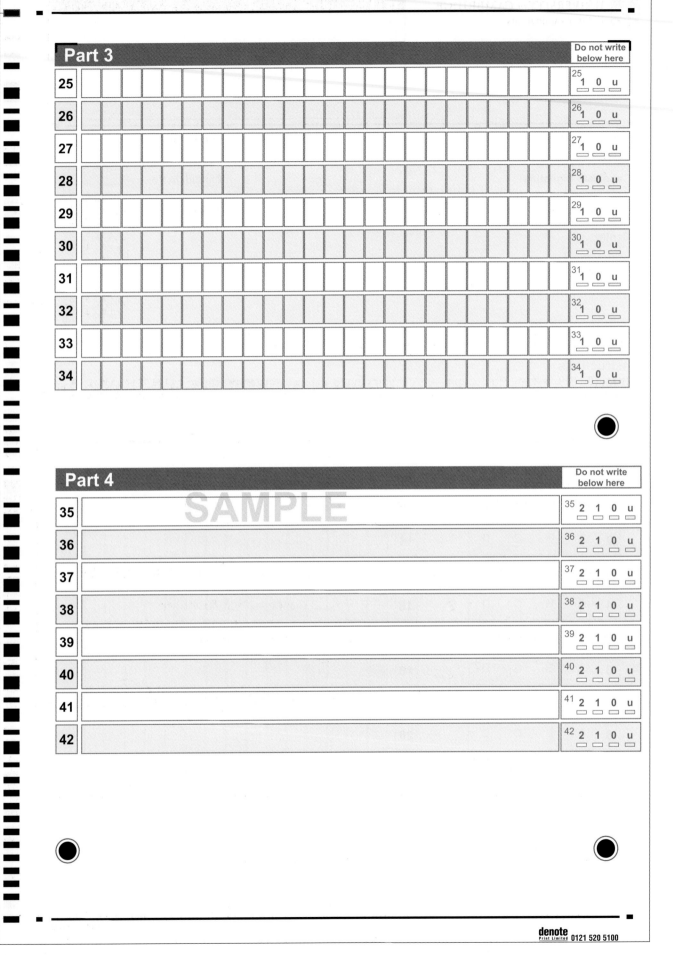

Part 3

													Do not write below here
25													25 1 0 u
26													26 1 0 u
27													27 1 0 u
28													28 1 0 u
29													29 1 0 u
30													30 1 0 u
31													31 1 0 u
32													32 1 0 u
33													33 1 0 u
34													34 1 0 u

Part 4

SAMPLE

	Do not write below here
35	35 2 1 0 u
36	36 2 1 0 u
37	37 2 1 0 u
38	38 2 1 0 u
39	39 2 1 0 u
40	40 2 1 0 u
41	41 2 1 0 u
42	42 2 1 0 u

denote Print Limited 0121 520 5100

UNIVERSITY of CAMBRIDGE
ESOL Examinations

Do not write in this box

Candidate Name
If not already printed, write name in CAPITALS and complete the Candidate No. grid (in pencil).

Candidate Signature

SAMPLE

Examination Title

Centre

Supervisor:
If the candidate is ABSENT or has WITHDRAWN shade here ▭

Centre No.

Candidate No.

Examination Details

0	0	0	0
1	1	1	1
2	2	2	2
3	3	3	3
4	4	4	4
5	5	5	5
6	6	6	6
7	7	7	7
8	8	8	8
9	9	9	9

Test version: A B C D E F J K L M N   Special arrangements: S H

Candidate Answer Sheet

Instructions

Use a PENCIL (B or HB).
Rub out any answer you wish to change using an eraser.

Parts 1, 3 and 4:
Mark ONE letter for each question.

For example, if you think **B** is the right answer to the question, mark your answer sheet like this:

Part 2:
Write your answer clearly in CAPITAL LETTERS.

Write one letter or number in each box.
If the answer has more than one word, leave one box empty between words.

For example:

Turn this sheet over to start.

FCE L

DP599/306

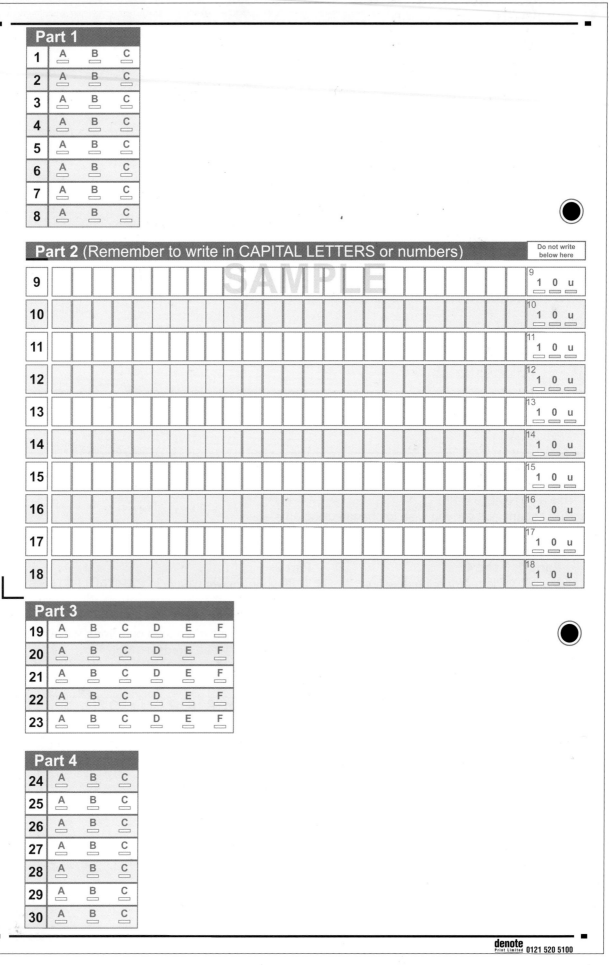

Part 1

1	A	B	C
2	A	B	C
3	A	B	C
4	A	B	C
5	A	B	C
6	A	B	C
7	A	B	C
8	A	B	C

Part 2 (Remember to write in CAPITAL LETTERS or numbers)

Do not write below here

9		9 1 0 u
10		10 1 0 u
11		11 1 0 u
12		12 1 0 u
13		13 1 0 u
14		14 1 0 u
15		15 1 0 u
16		16 1 0 u
17		17 1 0 u
18		18 1 0 u

SAMPLE

Part 3

19	A	B	C	D	E	F
20	A	B	C	D	E	F
21	A	B	C	D	E	F
22	A	B	C	D	E	F
23	A	B	C	D	E	F

Part 4

24	A	B	C
25	A	B	C
26	A	B	C
27	A	B	C
28	A	B	C
29	A	B	C
30	A	B	C

denote Print Limited 0121 520 5100